# HELL COMES TO SOUTHERN MARYLAND

The Story of Point Lookout Prison and
Hammond General Hospital

Bradley M. Gottfried and Linda I. Gottfried

Turning Point Publishing
Fairfield, Pennsylvania

Copyright © 2018 by Bradley M. Gottfried and Linda I. Gottfried

All rights reserved. No part of this publication may be reproduced, stored in a retrieval system, or transmitted, in any form or by any means electronic, mechanical, photocopying, recording, or otherwise, without the prior written permission of the authors.

ISBN-13: 978-0692128640

Library of Congress Control Number: 2018907611

Published by Turning Point Publishing

This publication is available at special discounts for bulk purchases. Send inquiries to bradgottfried@yahoo.com.

Printed in the United States of America

This book is lovingly dedicated to our parents

Bernice and Edward Gottfried

Joan and Michael Voglis

and

the men and women who worked, lived and died at
Point Lookout Prisoner of War Camp

# Table of Contents

Introduction ................................................................................................. 1

Chapter 1: A Hospital Grows in Southern Maryland ..................................... 5

Chapter 2: A Prison Takes Shape ................................................................ 12

Chapter 3: Point Lookout Prison Grows in Size and Population ................ 23

Chapter 4: Who Was Imprisoned at Point Lookout? ................................... 26

Chapter 5: How Prisoners Got to Point Lookout
Prisoner of War Camp................................................................................. 28

Chapter 6: Conditions in the Camp ............................................................ 31

Chapter 7: Passing the Time ....................................................................... 59

Chapter 8: Guarding the Prisoners ............................................................. 72

Chapter 9: How prisoners could leave Point Lookout ................................ 79

Chapter 10: Military Actions Associated with
Point Lookout Prison .................................................................................. 87

Chapter 11: The Forts or Redoubts............................................................. 91

Chapter 12: Discipline, Death and Misery.................................................. 93

Chapter 13: Prison Leadership ................................................................. 101

Chapter 14: The End of Point Lookout Prisoner of War Camp ............... 104

Chapter 15: How Many Confederates Died at Point Lookout? ............... 107

Chapter 16: Why the North Believed Their Treatment of
Point Lookout Prisoners was Justified ..................................................... 110

Chapter 17: Point Lookout after the War................................................. 113

Appendix 1: The Galvanized Yankees ..................................................... 117

Appendix 2: The Fall and Rise of Prisoner Exchanges and Paroles........ 122

Bibliography ............................................................................................. 124

Index.......................................................................................................... 127

# Introduction

A book concerning the Point Lookout Prisoner of War Camp is not easy to write. Wars are bloody affairs ending with one side the victor and the other vanquished. Civil Wars by nature have the added dimension of passionate philosophical differences. These intense conflicts simmer over years until they burst into a fiery fight. Although one side wins, both combatants engage in an ardent struggle after the war to justify their cause in an effort to ensure their behavior is not further criticized. This is especially true of American's Civil War.

The treatment of prisoners of war became a hot topic after the conclusion of hostilities. Each side vilified and criticized the other to convince everyone they provided the best possible treatment of prisoners under their care. Professor James Gillispie wrote in his recent book, *Andersonvilles of the North*, "Both Northerners and Southerners in the half-century or so following the war exploited this issue for personal, political, and social reasons." A skewed example was attempted by the historian of the 4th Rhode Island Infantry who disingenuously wrote, "It would seem that with plenty of food, clothing and good quarters, this [Point Lookout Prisoner of War Camp] was a desirable place for them to stay. The mortality from disease was very small. As soon as reported sick they were removed to the large field hospital on the point, and shared equally with our own sick men the benefits and blessings which a humane government afforded, and when they died were buried with a soldier's honors." Every segment of this statement is false and prompts questions about the writer's motivation.

Attacks on the other side's abuse of prisoners were more common. Outrage about the plight of Union prisoners at Andersonville began even before the war ended. Photographs of soldiers looking like living skeletons shock and disturb to this day. These graphic images affected how Union authorities interacted with the Confederacy. Treatment of prisoners at Union-run camps, such as Point Lookout also concerned the Confederate government and humanitarian organizations alike, prompted requests for inspections. Conditions at the camps exploded into hundreds of condemning articles, memoirs, and books after the war.

The Confederate Andersonville and Libby prisons were criticized for their inhumane treatment of Northern soldiers. Circumstances at these prisons were used to characterize Southerners as "fiendish, immoral, and un-Christian barbarians." The historian of the 4th Rhode Island Infantry proclaimed: "Thus it will be seen that while our Union prisoners in the horrible pens of the South were starving and dying by hundreds and thousands from hunger and exposure, the rebel prisoners under our charge were treated with nearly the same amount of food, clothing, and medical care as our own troops in active service."

Many former Confederate soldiers countered with accounts of how they too were regularly abused in Union prisons. Prisoners starving in "a land of plenty" were common themes. One wrote, "The Federal Government was rich, its resources unlimited and it had the entire world to draw upon. If there was an exercise of inhumanity, the Confederate government may have had an excuse. The Federal government had none." These men tried to justify the inadequate supplies provided to prisoners in Southern prisons as the result of the Union blockade that had cut off supplies and lost territory meant fewer crops for anyone living in the South. This view posits the challenge of inadequate supplies, not any conscious desire to harm their charges.

These excuses did not eliminate the accusations against the Confederacy, so hundreds of writers in the 50 years after Robert E. Lee's surrender sought to prove "the sufferings of the Confederate prisoners in Northern 'prison pens' were terrible beyond description; they were starved in a land of plenty; they were frozen where fuel and clothing were abundant; they suffered untold horrors for want of medicine, hospital stores, and proper medical attention; they were shot by sentinels, beaten by officers, and subjected to the most cruel punishments upon the slightest pretext…" according to a modern author.

This brings us to the difficulty of writing this book—many former prisoners' accounts *could have been* embellished as a way of striking back at Northern criticism of the Andersonville and Libby prisons. Reports of plenty of food contrast with scarcity; adequate clothes and blankets are contradicted by reports of men clad in rags, and several men sharing one blanket. We have addressed these contradictions by concentrating on period diaries and letters—a less politically charged source. We used a wealth of resources in writing this book, but gave more credence to those period observations in diaries, letters, and general orders.

Many modern historians believe both governments could have better treated prisoners of war under their care. James Gillespie took the position that "Union policies towards Confederate prisoners were more humane than commonly thought," but Charles Sanders's book, *While in the Hands of the Enemy*, posited a harsher point of view: leadership "increasingly came to regard prisoners not as men, but mere pawns to be used and then callously discarded in pursuit of national objectives."

We will examine the conditions at Point Lookout with these divergent opinions as a backdrop. While the intent of this book is to describe the camp, it is impossible to do so without becoming entangled in controversy.

Many prisons housed captured Confederate soldiers, actually almost forty. Most were small, but the largest were: Fort Delaware; Johnson's Island (Ohio), Camp Chase (Ohio); Camp Morton (Indiana), Camp Douglas (Illinois), Rock Island (Illinois), and Elmira (New York). The largest of all was Point Lookout, but it has generated little scholarly work compared with the other prisons. After a thorough review of the conditions at Union prisoner of war camps, James Gillispie wrote "if ever there was a 'Northern Andersonville,' Point Lookout was certainly in the running for that title."

Finally, we wrote this book because we love Southern Maryland. Although transplants, we have embraced the rich history and culture of the region. While several books have been written about Point Lookout Prison, the coverage has been extensive and esoteric. We present this modest volume to reach a wider audience.

A number of individuals assisted in completing this book. Pete Himmelheber, Bill Moody, Dan Toomey, and T. J. Youhn reviewed the manuscript and provided valuable insights. Frankie Tippett and the folks at the

St. Mary's Historical Society assisted in the research. Ed Cheney and Dr. Julie King shared their Point Lookout study. Edwin Beitzell's book on Point Lookout was a significant source of information and inspiration. A portion of the net sales will be donated to the St. Mary's Historical Society, which does such a great job of honoring St. Mary's history, and to the Friends of Point Lookout who are the guardians of the site and help keep its history alive.

# Chapter 1
## A Hospital Grows in Southern Maryland

The Southern tip of St. Mary's County, later known as Point Lookout was first settled by Native Americans. The arrival of Father Andrew White, S.J. in 1634, encouraged white settlers to move to the area. Clashes quickly flared, including at least one where a father was scalped and his two sons kidnapped. In June of 1681 between five and seven colonists were killed. The area was frequently used by disembarking British military during the Revolutionary War and the War of 1812.

War came again to America in 1861. The clouds of discord were seeded as early as the founding of our Country when issues of slavery and states' rights went unresolved. By 1863, or a full two years into the war, both sides hardened and locked in a death grip. As the fighting settled into what increasingly appeared to be a long-term struggle producing multitudes of casualties, the U.S. authorities realized additional hospital beds were a necessity. With the ever shifting location of combat, it became clear that large, permanent hospital facilities could not be located in Virginia. Accessibility and availability became two important criteria to site a new hospital complex. Point Lookout on the southern tip of St. Mary's County, Maryland "dotted all of the I's." Located on a spit of land between the Chesapeake Bay and the Potomac River, it was an easy boat ride from Virginia, so the wounded could easily be shifted there for long-term treatment. Medical professionals also liked the open, sunny, and breezy location they thought would aid in the healing process. Equally important, the owner of the property was anxious to do business with the Government.

The planners of the prison didn't know the site was highly exposed, and as a result, was exceptionally cold in the winter and hot in the summer. Flooding was also an issue. In addition, abundant marshes dotting the point were a breeding ground for mosquitoes that carried and spread disease. A prisoner recalled that the land at Point Lookout was "utterly innocent of trees, shrubs, or any natural equivalent of the same."

The future site of the Point Lookout out prison and medical facilities during the eighteenth century and early part of the nineteenth was equally inhospitable to the few trying to eke out a living. When the U.S. Government decided to build a series of coastal lighthouses, Point Lookout was high on the list. Built in 1830, the lighthouse remains in operation today. Fast forward to the summer of 1857 when William Cost Johnson, a former Congressman, purchased 400 acres of land for the purpose of establishing a sea-side resort. Construction of a number of buildings immediately commenced as wealthy individuals signed up to lease land for cabins and larger homes. All who visited the Point realized it could be a wonderful place to spend the summer. By 1859, 44 subscribers had committed, including the Chief Justice of the U.S., a wealthy inventor, and a U.S. Congressman. While most were from Maryland and Washington, D.C., some came from as far as Chicago and New Orleans. The resort eventually boasted a two-story frame hotel, a steamboat wharf and at least one hundred cottages.

A number of issues conspired against the continued success of this new resort. First, Johnson died on April 14, 1860 and his heirs were saddled with a project they did not want. Second, when the war came, interest in summer cottages waned, forcing the project into financial distress. William Allen of Baltimore agreed to purchase the land, but only if Johnson's heirs agreed to provide the mortgage. Believing this to be a stroke of luck, they agreed to unload what they thought to be a financial albatross. What they didn't know, but Allen may have, was the U.S. Government was seeking to lease land for hospitals and Point Lookout high was on the list.

The U.S. Surgeon General, Dr. W. A. Hammond, ordered an inspection of the property and subsequently filed a recommendation with Quartermaster

General, M.C. Meigs on June 5, 1862: "I have had them inspected by a Surgeon of experience, and his report is very favorable to their occupation. It is estimated that they will accommodate from 1,300 to 1,500 men besides ample room for quarters, storehouses, dispensary, kitchens, etc." Hammond was referring to the 100 cottages and large hotel which sat empty.

Hammond received good news on July 17, 1862 when Meigs gave permission to "proceed at once to the construction of the hospital." The medical personnel in Baltimore were initially tasked with supplying food, contracting with physicians to staff the wards, finding horses and wagons to move patients, and securing necessary furniture. They were told to "take with you three assistants and a sufficient number of citizen nurses from other hospitals." They could also request a number of Sisters of Charity to help minister to the sick and wounded. As many as 25 nuns worked at the hospital by the end of 1862. One Sister, Consolata Conlan, died of Typhoid Fever in August, 1862. Unlike others who died in the prison, she was placed in a simple coffin, rather than being buried in a sheet. She was given full military honors as the procession marched solemnly to her final resting place under a grove of trees near the Potomac River. Perhaps realizing the existing buildings would not be sufficient to handle the onrush of sick and wounded, Hammond requested the services of Capt. L.C. Edwards, Assistant Quartermaster to design and build a new facility. Hammond General Hospital became one of the largest medical facilities in the North. Part of the lease agreement with Allen required the new facilities to be built by his crews; the supplies and building materials provided by the Government. The dire needs of medical facilities dictated a rapid pace of construction. Until the facilities were complete, the existing hotel and cottages were pressed into service as wards and auxiliary structures. The first group of patients arrived on August 17, 1862 aboard the steamer, *State of Maine*. As the 350 wounded and sick Union troops walked or were carried off the ship, the wharf collapsed. No lives were lost and construction immediately began on a sturdy 280 by 16 foot wharf later expanded by 30 feet when Point Lookout became a supply depot.

Rather than one large building, the hospital wards were laid out in 16 wings to take advantage of the bright airy conditions. Fifteen, 175 by 25 foot wards housed patients; a sixteenth wider structure served as an office for physicians.

Thirty-six feet separated each building, which radiated out like the spokes of a wheel. The wards connected by an inner circular corridor, measured eight feet wide and a hundred feet long, allowing easy movement to all 16 buildings. The hospital housed 1,400 beds. Four interconnected buildings, attached to the inner circle, sat in the middle of the building complex, featuring a chapel, kitchen, library, and baggage room. A 20,000 gallon water tank was situated in the center of the circle to provide water for patients and for fire suppression, if the need arose. The hospital's design was considered quite revolutionary at the time as it traded one large building for several smaller ones, each with lots of surface area to allow maximum light and fresh air.

Caring for 1,400 patients and facilitating hundreds of hospital personnel required additional spaces. These functions were accommodated via more than 50 auxiliary buildings including personnel quarters, laundry, bakeries, stables, saddleries, post office, and storehouses. Because of frequent high tides and flooding, the hospital facility was set on piles, two to three feet above grade. The new hospital became the "Hammond General Hospital" in honor of the Surgeon General from Maryland.

Although all the surgeons and most nurses were men, a number of women were employed during the war. Sarah Blunt wrote on March 26, 1864, that she received 40 cents a day and rations. Medical personnel were also provided with living quarters because of the isolated location of the hospital.

Union soldiers came and went until 1863 when Confederate soldiers were added to the wards. A report that 6,000–10,000 wounded Confederates needed care after the battle of Gettysburg prompted Federal soldiers convalescing there to be transferred to Baltimore hospitals. Prison authorities scrambled to increase the hospital's capacity, again requisitioning the hotel and cottages as wards. They added 1,300 to 1,500 beds to the 1,400 beds in the actual hospital wards. The increase did not stop concern, as they were told to expect as many as 8,000–10,000 wounded. The wards overflowed with patients during 1864 and 1865 because of an abundance of Confederate sick that overwhelmed the facilities. Authorities coped with the numbers by establishing smaller facilities outside of the hospital for specific needs (see

Chapter 11- Sick and Dying). The hospital did a reasonable job of handling the sick and wounded. Capt. Henry Dickinson, afflicted with cholera, spent a week in the hospital and later wrote he "received every attention that I desired." He commented on the availability of medicine and a "sick diet furnished in abundance."

The first death, J. McLaughlin, of the 9th Massachusetts Infantry occurred soon after the prison opened; the last death occurred on July 25, 1865, when a soldier by the name of "Davis" died. The youngest soldier to die at the hospital was 16-year old John Leery of the 88th Pennsylvania who was wounded on February 6, 1865.

Prior to May 8, 1862, authorities in Washington did not give much thought to handling the Union soldiers who died at the hospital. This changed when Surgeon General Hammond wrote to Meigs: "the graveyard is without fence or protection, the graves only marked through the kindness of friends or the ward masters; not a single properly marked headboard has been put up by the Quartermaster." It did not take long—a bit more than a month—for changes to occur. Each grave was marked with a headboard bearing the deceased's name, rank, company, and regiment. The grave yard was kept separate from those of Confederate dead, and was located on the northwest side of the prisoners' stockade.

A newspaper, *The Hammond Gazette,* was published by hospital staff. It contained a wealth of information, such as lists of sick and wounded soldiers housed at other hospitals, visits by dignitaries, such as Abraham Lincoln (who visited on December 17, 1863) and Secretary of State William Seward, and deaths among the patients. The paper was published for almost two years.

Although the war ended in April, 1865, the patients remained. On May 16, 1865, the commander of the district reported 1,700 of the 1,859 Confederate patients were well enough to go home. By July 5, all but a few were released and the hospital closed on July 15, 1865.

Close up of Hammond General Hospital

Dr. W. A. Hammond, Surgeon General

Prison outbuildings and officers' quarters. Point Lookout was transformed into a small town during the Civil War, containing sevreal hospitals, warehouses, wharfs, stables, service buildings, and staff quarters.

# Chapter 2
## A Prison Takes Shape

### Increasing Prison Populations

The reason the prison population exploded after mid-1863 is beyond the scope of this small book, but some background information must be shared to provide context for the camp conditions.

Early in the war, Quartermaster General, Montgomery Meigs urged Secretary of War, Simon Cameron, to create and administer a prison system to deal with enemy captives. In October 1861, Col. William Hoffman was appointed Commissary-General of Prisoners. Meigs believed prisoners "are entitled to proper accommodations [and] to courteous and respectful treatment," but he also worried about excessive spending on prisoners. Between 1861 to mid-1863, prisoner of war camps were largely holding areas for soldiers until they could be exchanged. A soldier might spend several months in captivity, but these camps were meant to be short-term solutions. After a battle, prisoners could be "exchanged" for an equal number of soldiers and officers captured by the other side, or simply paroled.

This created some difficulties. For example, Robert E. Lee almost lost the battle of Antietam (September, 1862) because an 8,000-man division was left behind to parole the garrison at Harpers Ferry. "Paroled" prisoners were released after promising never to take up arms against the enemy until properly exchanged. Many former prisoners immediately violated their paroles and re-entered the army. By 1863 both governments fretted over paroles becoming "get out of the army" tickets. Soldiers no longer wishing to serve, could throw up their arms and surrender, be paroled and then head home, never to serve again. Both sides tried to avoid paroles in favor of "exchanges," which returned the prisoners to their respective armies.

The exchange of prisoners was directed by an agreement or Cartel. When the war began in 1861 both sides believed it would be a short, largely bloodless affair. When the initial battles came and went without either side giving in, both governments knew it would be a protracted war. The two sides hammered out the Cartel in 1862. The Cartel specified the value of each type of soldier: an army commander was worth 60 privates, a major general for 40 privates, a brigadier general for 20, a colonel for 15, etc.

As the armies became larger and the number of prisoners multiplied, new prisons were built and the Federal Government issued General Orders Number 100 in April, 1863 to ensure uniformity among the camps. The General Order lasted only a month, for the Cartel ended on May 20, 1863 and remained dormant until just before the conclusion of the war. The Cartel ended for a variety of reasons, but decaying relations between the two governments was most important. Communication became increasingly contentious and prison conditions were often the cause of the disputes. Questions about unequal exchanges, and "cheating"—Confederate prisoners were returning to their units before being formally exchanged also became an issue. The U.S. Government posed questions about the treatment of their soldiers which the South took as an affront to its honor.

Secretary of War Edwin Stanton claimed the Cartel ended because of the South's refusal to include captured African American soldiers and their white officers in the exchange process. These men would instead be put to death. By ending the Cartel, Stanton hoped to soften the South's position on the treatment of these troops.

Occasional exchanges and paroles occurred after this point, but it was not until early 1865 as the end of the war grew near, the two sides finally agreed to reinstate the exchanges. For at least 15 months, prisoners were caught in the middle and suffered mightily. Many thousands died and more were maimed for the rest of their lives. In February, 1865, 10,000 Confederate prisoners were exchanged from Northern camps, and another 14,000 the following month. This was too little, too late, for the war would end in April. (More information on exchanges and paroles can be found in Appendix 2.)

## Creating the Point Lookout Prisoner of War Camp

The large number of Confederate prisoners captured at Gettysburg, Pennsylvania and Vicksburg, Mississippi threatened to over-whelm the Union prisons already in existence. On July 20, 1863, Gen. Meigs ordered the creation of a new prisoner of war camp at Point Lookout. He reasoned that up to 10,000 prisoners could be maintained at the camp, relying on tents to house the men. Few permanent facilities would be constructed. He may have rationalized the climate in Southern Maryland eliminated the need for more hardy shelters, but he was wrong. The area sustained blistering heat in the summer and icy winds in the winter. According to Col. Hoffman, the site was selected because of its isolation and ease of defense from Confederate attack. Point Lookout became the *only* Northern prison that did not house the Confederate prisoners in wooden barracks.

The decision to house prisoners at Point Lookout demanded a myriad of actions. First, the prison had to be planned and built. General-in-Chief Henry Halleck wrote on July 23, 1863, "Tents, lumber for kitchens, cooking apparatus, &c., have already been ordered to that place by the quartermaster's department. The camp should be so laid out that it can be extended sufficiently to accommodate about 10,000 prisoners."

Part of the planning process was how to defend the prison. Guard units were identified and the navy was called to patrol the waters around the camp to prevent escapes or rescue attempts. Just a few days after the decision to house prisoners at Point Lookout, Secretary of War, Gideon Wells issued an order to Commodore A.A. Harwood, commander of the Washington Naval Yard and the Potomac Flotilla: "you will direct a sufficient naval force to be always in close vicinity and in communication with the senior army officer at that point."

St. Mary's County now merited its own military district because of the complexity of the activities occurring there, particularly at Point Lookout.

A few days after, July 23, 1863, the decision to create what became known as Camp Hoffman (after Colonel William Hoffman, the Federal Commissary General of Prisoners); St. Mary's County was detached from the Middle Department. Brigadier General Gilman Marston was warned by Halleck that "the strictest guard must be kept over the prisoners and also order, discipline, and cleanliness in their camp."

## The First Prisoners Arrive

Union authorities wasted no time in populating the camp. Col. Hoffman sent 800 prisoners from Baltimore and another 500 from Washington's Old Capitol Prison in July. Maj. Gen. E. A. Hitchcock visited the camp on August 31, 1863 and reported a total of 1,800 prisoners and 400 guards. As prisoners were sent from other overcrowded facilities, the numbers swelled to almost 4,000 by the end of September, 1863, and to more than 9,000 by the end of 1863.

By the end of the war Point Lookout would be known as the largest prisoner of war camp in the North, housing as many as 52,000 Confederates at one time or another. In addition, another 301 political prisoners, including a number of women, were incarcerated. There was not adequate time to plan, as prisoners began arriving almost as soon as the prison was established.

The prison was woefully unprepared to accept its first 1,300 prisoners in July. The lack of a stockade (work would not begin on it until October 8, 1863), caused the guards to form a human wall around the prisoners, housed in tents. The number of prisoners rose to 7,600 by October, and with concerns about winter, Marston sent recommendations for construction of a permanent camp in October, 1863. His request included building wooden barracks for the prisoners. He knew Maryland winters could be severe. The ground would be soft and wet during the rainy season and the dampness infiltrated the tents. To make the idea of spending money for permanent structures more palatable, Marston reasoned the permanent structures would actually save money, as the prisoners would build the structures themselves and firewood use would be dramatically reduced. The recommendations went up the ladder and were approved at each level until they reached Sec. of War Edwin Stanton who rejected them. Let the prisoners occupy tents, he wrote. Not only would Point

Lookout be the largest prison in the North, it would also be the only one that relied on tents to house prisoners. Stanton never explained his reasoning, but some have hypothesized he erroneously believed Southern Maryland was fairly temperate in the winter and wooden enclosures were not necessary. The living quarters of the guards—also tents—suggests ignorance rather than maliciousness may have prevailed, at least in this case.

Tents to house large numbers of men were needed, but not readily available. By the end of October, 1863, a tent city began to take shape. The tents were often army cast-offs and whatever was available at the time. The tents included antiquated French bell tents, A-tents, wall tents, Sibley tents, and hospital fly tents. J.B. Stamp noted the men were "quartered in what were apparently old army tents, of many shapes and sizes." Fully a third of the tents were unfit for use in the field, so they were sent to Point Lookout. Many were full of holes and leaked when it rained; others were flimsy because of their rotting material. The Sibley type of tent was the most common and it fit the bill as each could accommodate as many as 14 men. As the number of men multiplied, the number of tents did not, and more and more men were crammed into the tents so every inch was taken up by human flesh. B.T. Holliday recalled a hundred men were housed in six tents, or about 17 men per tent. This elicited pleas from prison authorities for additional tents—which occasionally came and sometimes didn't. (See Chapter 6: Conditions in the Camp.)

## The Prison Forms its Own Hospital
As the prison population grew, so too did the demand for beds in Hammond General Hospital. This growth forced establishment of auxiliary medical facilities to treat minor illnesses or act as holding tanks until beds became available. By November, 1863, the prison's medical facilities consisted of 18 hospital tents, placed in two rows, with a broad street between them. The number of tents increased to 30 a month later. As conditions at the camp worsened, these facilities became swamped with seriously ill prisoners.

## Layout of the Prisoner of War Camp
All Civil War prisoner of war camps shared a number of features. The pens holding the prisoners were the most important, but there were other

important components, including commissary storehouses, camps and recreational facilities for the guards, stables, machine shops, and anything needed to support a community of prisoners that exceeded 20,000 men toward the end of the war. Camp authorities created a smallpox hospital, about three-quarters of a mile north of the camp, near Point Lookout Creek. Because of the virulence of this disease, which could kill as many as 75 percent of those infected, it was situated far from the prisoner pens and guards' camps.

Point Lookout sported two prison pens: one 20 acres in size; the other 10 acres. The larger prison pen consisted of double rows of tents, back-to-back and 20-foot wide avenues running in front of each row. There were initially 10 streets, with a drainage ditch running along each side. By the end of the war, the number of streets increased to 20, which meant almost the entire pen was taken up by tents and mess halls (see below). It is difficult to imagine 20,000 men crammed into such a small space. In modern terms, a typical football field spans 1.32 acres. That means the prison pen was the equivalent of 15 football fields, leaving little space for recreational purposes.

The prison pens were surrounded by 14 foot high board fences made of two inch wide planks buried a couple of feet into the ground to prevent tunneling. Therefore, the fence was about 12 feet above the ground. A walkway was built on the outside of the fence, close to its top, three feet wide, encircling the camp. Here guards walked their beat, looking down on the prisoners to ensure order and discouraged escape. Guards stationed about every 40 feet in good weather, used a shelter every hundred feet during inclement weather.

The prisoners could not approach the wall because of the "deadline." A shallow ditch was dug about ten feet from the wall and any prisoner crossing it would be shot on sight. The guards yelled down to a prisoner who crossed the line and warned him to "move back or be shot." Some ignored the command because of their despair and some may not have heard the guard. Rookie guards occasionally forgot to give the command and opened fire without warning. Private Leon Lewis of North Carolina recorded in his diary on May 23, 1864: "We are not allowed to cross a certain line, called the deadline, but as many as 500 men go at one time to meals [see below], of course near the door there is always a rush. Today one of our men accidentally crossed the line. He was pushed over by the crowd, when a black devil shot and killed him, and wounded two others."

There were several gates built into the enclosure. Some led to the beaches on the Chesapeake Bay and the wharf there; others were on the Potomac River used for wagons. These will be discussed later.

Six mess halls were constructed to serve the men. Unlike the tents, these were elevated 3-4 feet off the ground to avoid flooding. Each wooden building ran 160 feet long and 22 feet wide, with about 20 feet used as the kitchen. The latter contained food preparation tables and four 50 gallon cauldrons to make soup or gruel. Three to five long tables ran the length of the eating area. As many as 500 men could be accommodated at a time, so the number of shifts increased along with the numbers of prisoners to be served. Rows of tin plates about 20 inches apart lined each table.

When the men filed into the mess halls, each halted in front of a plate with food. When all were assembled they grabbed the contents and immediately left the building, eating as they walked. The sergeants and cook staff constantly watched the men to make sure they were not taking anything other than what was on their plates. There was no sitting and eating—just grab and go. When soup or coffee was served, the men quickly downed the liquid and then walked off. Point Lookout was the only Federal prison with mess halls, probably because the men ate in their barracks in the other facilities.

A second pen, ten-acre in size, was originally dedicated to Confederate officers incarcerated at Point Lookout. The camp's medical facilities were initially located between the two pens. When the officers were transferred to Fort Delaware, beginning in June, 1864, the smaller pen was given over to expanded medical facilities.

According to the historian of the 5th New Hampshire Infantry, which guarded the camp during the first year of operation, another prisoner encampment was established. This one, north of its camp, and at the furthest extreme of the camp, was for "Galvanized Yankees"—those prisoners who had taken the oath of allegiance and agreed to serve in the U.S. armed forces (see Chapter 9: "How prisoners could leave the prison" and Appendix 1).

Federal authorities attempted to keep order in the prison pens by organizing the prisoners into companies and divisions. A hundred men were assigned to each company and each division contained 10 companies or a thousand prisoners. Each street comprised a division. Two Confederate sergeants were assigned to each company and a Federal sergeant to each division.

Being named a company sergeant was a much sought after position by the prisoners because it gave them a measure of authority and freer access to the mess hall facilities. As a result, none of these sergeants were emaciated. One was the "Company Sergeant" who conducted roll call, inspected the tents and the men and generally oversaw their activities. The other was the "Sick Sergeant," who reported the lists of the sick and carried their rations to them at the sick tents next to the prison pen.

A newspaper reporter visited the camp when it was almost a year old and published his observations on May 6, 1864:

> *On entering one sees only a confused mass of tents and houses, and men hurrying to and from, and hears a medley of sounds not unlike the hum of a city business street, for the entrance gate opens upon a plaza or main street, running the length of the lot, on which are situated the cookhouses, commissary building, sutler's store and post office. Around these crowds linger from reveille to retreat. Into this street empty, at regular intervals, cross streets leading the width of the lot, and long them on either side, arranged with military exactness, the dwellings of the prisoners- tents or cracker box houses . . .*

Secretary of War, Edwin Stanton
Stanton was known for being a strong proponent
of creating conditions at Union prisoner of war camps
to retaliate against conditions at Confederate prison camps

Quartermaster General Montgomery Meigs
Meigs played a major role in keeping the supplies rolling
which were so important to the Union's ultimate success

Brigadier General Gilman Marston
First commander of the Point Lookout Prisoner of War Camp

Commissary-General of Prisoners, Col. William Hoffman
Hoffman oversaw all Northern prisoner of war camps.
Known for his frugality, he contributed to the prisoners' misery

Close-up of Prison Pens and Guard Camps

Prisoners Cook House
John Jacob Omenhausser sketchbook, 1864-1865, Maryland Manuscripts Collection, #5213, Special Collections, University of Maryland Libraries

# Chapter 3
## Point Lookout Prison Grows in Size and Population

**How the prison population changed during the war:**
The number of prisoners housed at Point Lookout Prison varied. The table was tabulated by the Federal Government. While some historians deem as inaccurate, it provides an indication of how the prison population fluctuated through the course of the war:

**1863**
| | |
|---|---|
| July | 136 |
| October | 7,585 |

**1864**
| | |
|---|---|
| January | 8,621 |
| April | 6,268 |
| July | 14,747 |
| October | 13,811 |

**1865**
| | |
|---|---|
| January | 11,860 |
| April | 20,110 |
| July | -- |

Overcrowding occurred almost from the camp's beginning. The camp experienced explosive growth during its earliest days, swelling from 136 in July to more than 7,500 by October of 1863. Prison numbers fluctuated and were related to the number of men transferred to other prisons, took the oath of alliance and were freed, or arrived because of great battles. The population more than doubled from April, 1864 to July, 1864 because of the major battles fought in Virginia (e.g., Overland Campaign) and in Georgia (e.g., Atlanta Campaign). Significant numbers of prisoner transfers occurred from time to time. For example, on March 12, 1864, a contingent of 4,000 prisoners was sent to Fort Delaware. The fort was deemed "a safer place for prisoners than Point Lookout" because of fear the Confederate government was contemplating a strike on the prison to free its men. The jump in numbers from April – July, 1864 also reflects the move of invalid prisoners from Johnson's Island and Baltimore to Point Lookout.

The summer of 1864 and the spring of 1865 were particularly difficult for all involved, for the number of prisoners doubled from the preceding quarter, straining supply systems, leading to wide-spread shortages and suffering (see Food). So many men (12,027) occupied the 20-acre prison pen in June, 1864, that the camp's surgeon, James Thompson was moved to "most respectfully protest against the reception of additional numbers of prisoners." He worried additional men would lead to "an epidemic that will decimate the ranks of prisoners." The plea had little impact, by the end of July; an additional 2,700 men were crammed into the pen.

In May, 1864, Col. Hoffman proclaimed 10,000 prisoners were housed at Point Lookout. He suggested, "5,000 more may be accommodated," but he was quick to add, "I do not think it would be advisable to assemble a greater number at this point." But assemble they did, and by the end of the war, more than 20,000 men would be crammed into the prison pens—far more than Hoffman felt could be supported.

Cracker Box used to line the bottom of tents for insulation against the cold and damp ground

# Chapter 4
## Who Was Imprisoned at Point Lookout?

Point Lookout was initially used as a processing center for Confederate prisoners, spending time here before being shuffled off to other prisons. With the ever-increasing number of Confederate prisoners, it transitioned to a traditional prison. Point Lookout initially housed Confederate soldiers of all ranks, but Confederate officers were transferred to Fort Delaware during the summer of 1864. The prison population reflected the composition of the Confederate armies as a whole. This meant a large number of men in their late teens and early 20's were incarcerated in the camp. On May 20, 1864, Col. Hoffman broke down the composition of the prisoners: 563 officers, 10,192 enlisted men and 192 citizens; in all, 10,947 prisoners.

While the majority of detainees were enlisted men, civilians were also incarcerated from time to time. About 250 civilians, mainly smugglers and political prisoners, were thrown into the prison during the course of its existence. Smuggling was a profitable business during the Civil War and boats constantly plied the Potomac River, bringing goods to be sold at exorbitant prices in Virginia. Capture meant a one-way ticket to the Old Capitol Prison or Point Lookout. Similarly, a number of civilians were arrested and incarcerated for their open support of the South. If too vocal, they too would be detained at Point Lookout Prison.

Not much is known about women prisoners, but there were a handful. Mary Gilliam and Kath Davidson were arrested for blockade running, on April 15, 1864, in Leonardtown, Maryland, and spent time at Point Lookout. Mrs. Hunter Davidson was arrested in Annapolis, Maryland, in January, 1864 for unknown reasons and sent to Point Lookout. Jane Perkins of Danville, Virginia, cut her hair and enlisted as a Confederate artilleryman at the age of 23. She may have been a teacher before the war and might have enlisted with her brother. She was captured two years later during a battle north of Richmond on May 27, 1864. Although she avoided detection for several years, the strip search upon her arrival at Point Lookout on June 8, 1864, exposed her gender. When questioned by the camp's provost marshal, she defiantly declared "she could straddle a horse, jump a fence, and kill a Yankee as well as any rebel." She was given her own small tent and then transferred on July 12, 1864 to Old Capital Prison and then to the Fitchburg (Massachusetts) Female Prison the following October. She was finally released in March 1865, and is lost to history.

African American Guard enforcing the "dead line"
John Jacob Omenhausser sketchbook, 1864-1865, Maryland Manuscripts Collection, #5213,
Special Collections, University of Maryland Libraries

# Chapter 5
## Getting to Point Lookout Prisoner of War Camp

The first step toward incarceration at Point Lookout Prison for most soldiers was capture on a battlefield. No one goes into battle expecting to be captured; it comes after a violent confrontation with the enemy. A soldier may have seen a number of his comrades killed or wounded and then a gun barrel or bayonet pointed in his face. Will the enemy soldier pull the trigger, ending his misery? Sometimes that happened, but more often, the soldier was ordered to drop his weapons and raise his hands in the air. Upon capture, Mississippian David Holt explained, "I cannot describe my feelings as we marched away from the battlefield, without guns, as prisoners of war."

The next step was getting the prisoners away from the battlefield. Active operations may be continuing, or the victorious army is following the vanquished enemy. Prisoners are usually an after-thought, whose safe removal is in the hands of the Provost Marshal. Prisoners were herded together on the battlefield and when the time came, marched to some unknown location. These marches might last days and cover as many as a hundred miles. Alabamian J.B. Stamp recalled he and the other prisoners waited 11 days until they were marched to Belle Plain, Virginia. They waited another three days for transportation and then hopped on steamers for Point Lookout.

The journey to Point Lookout was primarily via steamer. Often crammed together, the prisoners were not informed of their destination and they feared for their safety. Always on their minds the safety of their loved ones at home and their comrades left behind. Rations were usually scant during these journeys and when it was available were often not consumed by sea-sick prisoners.

Upon arrival, the prisoners, called "fresh fish" by the guards, were either assembled on the pier or just off of it, often formed in a square. They were told to "unwrap, spread out, and disgorge anything we had," according to a captured artilleryman. Another soldier opined all clothes except those close to the skin were removed and laid on the ground in front of them. Additional blankets and clothes were removed. A prisoner recalled the Union noncommissioned officer yelling, "Now, men, if you have anything valuable about your person or effects in the way of watches, jewelry, or money, we give you an opportunity to turn it over to us, and we will put your name on it and deposit it at the Provost Marshall's office and give you a certificate of deposit; and when you leave this prison, either on exchange or release, and present your certificate, we will return the goods left in our charge." Many prisoners claimed the goods were not forthcoming on release because "they could not be found."

Valuables were removed for several reasons. Money and other valuables could be used to bribe the guards or could be stolen by other prisoners (see below). Anything with "U.S." on it was also confiscated because it could be used to trick the guards during an escape attempt or used while a prisoner was on the lamb. It is unclear why extra blankets and clothing were confiscated, but may have been distributed to other prisoners in need.

Captain Henry Dickinson arrived at the Point Lookout wharf on a steamer at 11:00 p.m. during the summer of 1864. He recalled, "Several companies of the Sons of Africa here met us, formed in two lines. We were marched between them and, after considerable delay . . . we were marched up to the office of . . . the provost marshal. Here they were searched, and all valuables were removed. "Hats were turned inside out, and so also of pockets; boots were pulled off, etc." With the search complete, the men marched to the prison pen and assigned a tent. They quickly became acquainted with their tent-mates, who provided information on camp routine and the "do's and don'ts" to ensure survival.

The prisoner of war camp at Point Lookout relied on tents to house the men. It was assumed the climate in Southern Maryland eliminated the need for more hardy shelters; however, the area sustained blistering heat in the summer and icy winds in the winter

# Chapter 6
## Camp Conditions

It is hard for any of us to imagine what it was like to be a prisoner in a 20 acre pen with almost 20,000 others. We know an abundance of togetherness existed, but the rest of the conditions are in question, mired in politics and sectional friction. The dilemma in writing this book was described in the introduction and will be explored in this section, illustrating the various points of view.

Another problem associated with truly understanding the conditions is because they often changed through time. The prison authorities constantly changed the rules and regulations, especially when it came to food and clothing. Much was driven by the political climate of the period. Conditions changed depending on the number of prisoners present. As can be seen in Chapter 3, this also varied greatly throughout the war. Therefore, what occurred in 1865 could be very different from 1863.

Stories of abuse of prisoners by both the U.S. and C.S. governments became increasingly strident in late 1863 and 1864, leading to inspections and calls for better treatment. A communication from Gen. Benjamin Butler to his Confederate counterpart on Christmas Day, 1863 discussing the exchange of prisoners contained this curious statement from Butler: "I do not mean to say that their ration is as large as our regularly issued ration, because of their state of entire inactivity, but it is in every respect of the same quality as those issued to the men generally. If you have any doubt of it, upon an examination of the condition of the men I send you, and upon hearing their statements, please suggest what, in your judgment, should be done further in their behalf."

# The Report of the U.S. Sanitary Commission

Upon hearing of the conditions at Point Lookout, the U.S. Sanitary Commission, a forerunner of the American Red Cross, conducted a thorough inspection. Although an independent agency, its report carried much weight in the public arena because they were based in the North and the inspections were conducted by physicians. Dr. William F. Swalm was assigned the task of carrying out the investigation of the Point Lookout prison. The report released on November 13, 1863, impartially examined both the prisoner of war camp and its associated camp prison (not the Hammond General Hospital). Dr. Swalm began his report by remarking: "The accommodations here were much better than I expected to find them and much more comfortable, yet they had by no means the best of care." But he ended it on a cautionary note: "It is in the quarters [prison pens] that we have the most complaint and suffering. Men of all ages and classes, descriptions and hues, with various colored clothing, all huddled together, forming a motley crew, which to be appreciated must be seen, and what the pen fails to describe the imagination must depict . . . ." In between, the report attempted to provide an impartial evaluation of the major components, many of which were found to be deficient.

The report laid blame squarely on the prison's administration. "It is our fault when the officer in command fails to place in charge someone. . . . capable of giving commands and seeing that they are enforced. I know that [the prisoners] are our enemies . . . . but now they are within our powers and are suffering."

This sparked outrage in Gen. Marston and Col. Hoffman and their staffs. A week after its release, Marston wrote, "Of the report I have to remark that one more disingenuous and false could not well have been made. It is surprising that the commission should employ agents so stupid or dishonest as the author of this report."

After questioning the validity of the report and then attempting to quash it, Hoffman begrudgingly began addressing the issues. To avoid such embarrassment in the future, he banned any further investigations by the

Sanitation Commission. Future inspections would be conducted by the Government and were deemed by some to be less impartial. The reports, with the Government's responses, are included for each category below.

A snapshot of conditions of the men in mid-1864 was provided by an observer who watched as 2,000 Point Lookout prisoners arrived at a new facility in Elmira, New York: "They wore all sorts of nondescript uniforms, and some had nothing on but drawers and shirts." The observer found them to be "pale and emaciated, hollow-eyed and dispirited in every act and movement." Many had been vaccinated against smallpox, but the injections were contaminated, so many exhibited "great sores, big enough, it seems to put your arm through."

**Food**

The quality and quantity of food greatly interested the prisoners, prison authorities, and U.S. Government officials. At its most basic level, nutritious food was needed to ensure men did not fall victim to disease and possibly die. Like so many conditions at Point Lookout, some prisoners believed the food was plentiful; others said they never had enough. As indicated above, this may relate to when a prisoner was incarcerated in Point Lookout.

Some prisoners found the quality and quantity of food was often quite good during the early stages of the prison camp. Four months after the camp opened in August, 1863, Brig. Gen. Marston wrote to Hoffman, the prisoners received "wholesome food sufficient to insure vigorous health." This was not true when Dr. William Swalm inspected the camp a few months later, in November, 1863 (see below). While he found the quality to be sufficient, he questioned the quantity served to the prisoners.

Through the war, and long after, the U.S. Government was criticized for not providing enough food to the prisoners. Col. Hoffman did not help himself in this regard, when he established a fund in July 1863 that came from reducing the prisoners' rations and selling the extra food back to the commissary. It was designed to provide funds for commodities not granted by the Government, such as vegetables, fruits, and construction materials. The fund was

33

administered by the commander of each prison, with the understanding they knew how best to use the money for the benefit of the prisoners. The Point Lookout fund grew to $65,000 by the end of November, 1863, and by the end of the war, the figure had grown to $544,556. The amount in the fund was $1,800,000 for all Union prisons. To provide perspective, a typical Union soldier was paid $12 a month. The growth of this fund contradicts the statement it was intended to improve the life of the prisoners and suggests it was a way to save money on the backs of the prisoners.

Also telling is Col. Hoffman's directive to his prison commanders: "It is not expected that anything more will be done to provide for the welfare of rebel prisoners than is absolutely necessary, and in directing or recommending expenditures [from the prison fund] for their benefit you will have this constantly in mind."

An outbreak of scurvy caused Gen. Marston to request permission to purchase "beets, carrots, turnips, cabbages, and the like," to supplement the men's diet. Hoffman agreed, provided the prison fund was used and as the amount of vegetables increased, other items should be reduced so "the cost will to some extent be refunded," but he added, "this is not a material consideration." This was apparently done, for Col. Hoffman admitted on March 22, 1864, "At Point Lookout some articles of the rations have been reduced below the scale, but this has been made up by the purchase of vegetables and other articles." The "scale" Hoffman referred to was the amount of food the prisoner received each day. The men were given a reduced meat and cracker allocation to pay for vegetables.

### The U.S. Sanitation Commission Report Regarding Food (Nov. 1863)
Dr. Swalm noted in his report: "I heard a great deal of complaint that they did not get enough to eat. They wanted more meat. What they did get they spoke of in the highest terms. On questioning some of them which they would prefer an increase of the rations or blankets, all concluded that they could get along with the ration if they could get blankets."

"LES MISERABLES DE POINT LOOKOUT"—CONFEDERATES FACING THEIR SECOND FIGHT, 1865

Swalm asked to see a typical ration and noted, "On being shown a ration, I do not think they receive half the amount of meat they are entitled to, but with the crackers, &c., given they cannot suffer at all from hunger. The ration to the well man is pork, 3 ounces; salt or beef, 4 ounces; hard-tack, 10 ounces; coffee, 1 pint; a day's ration. Soup is also given once a week; potatoes and beans every five days; soft bread once a week, and fresh meat had been issued to them once a week up to two weeks ago, when from some cause unable to find out it was stopped."

He thought the cooking arrangements were adequate, but complained about how well the prison cooks prepared their meals. The bottom line from the report: The prisoners were receiving adequate quantities of food, but the variety and quality of its nutritional value were questionable.

## The Prison Authority's Response

Although the Commission's report was fairly complimentary on the quantity of food provided to the prisoners, Gen. Marston refuted the report, explaining to Col. Hoffman for the month of November, "the allowance per man was 13.3 ounces of bread, 8.1 ounces of meats, of vegetables and molasses the full ration; a pint of coffee on the days when soup is served and on other days a quart." Sergeant J. H. Wilkinson reported to Gen. Marston the men also received "bean or other soups are issued on an average once in three days; coffee twice a day--a pint at each time to every man excepting when soup is served, and all the vegetables and molasses that are allowed by the Army."

It is also interesting to note the prisoners were receiving vegetables during this period and Wilkinson claimed, "I never knew a time during my service when Federal troops got so constant a supply of vegetables as has been issued to the prisoners here." They neglected to mention the prison authorities were forced to provide more fruits and vegetables to combat the outbreak of scurvy.

## Conditions in the Camp after the Reports, and Prisoners' Observations

A reporter from the *New York Herald* reported early in 1864 (before the retaliations—see below) prisoners were given two meals a day: 8:00 a.m. and 3:00 p.m. For breakfast, the prisoners received, "a tin cup of coffee, with the addition of a spoonful of molasses once, or sometimes twice, a week." For dinner, the men received, "a piece of meat, either pork, pickled beef or fresh beef, the size of the piece varying from a quarter to three-quarters of a pound weight, and either coffee or soup . . . a pint to a man." He noted that a loaf of bread, "nine or ten ounces" was issued to each man. Sometimes crackers were substituted for the bread.

Rations were cut several times after Dr. Swalm's inspection. Gone were days with almost half a pound of meat, to be replaced with about half that amount. The reduction in rations appeared to be the direct result of retaliation caused by conditions at Southern prisons. The new retaliatory measures were publicized on April 20, 1864, and went after the easiest target—the prisoners' food. This was precisely what was being denied to the Union prisoners in Southern prisons.

Col. Hoffman contacted Sec. of War Stanton on May 19, 1864: "The ration as now issued to [the] prisoners of war may be considerably reduced without depriving them of the food necessary to keep them in health." After conferring with his staff, Stanton gave the go ahead and the reductions occurred on June 1, 1864. The total reductions amounted to 20% of an already meager ration. According to historian Roger Pickenpaugh, "Retaliation was now the policy of the Union."

The U.S. Sanitary Commission received a stream of reports suggesting the men were being starved and petitioned Gen. Meigs for an explanation.

His July 6, 1864 response indicates rations had indeed been reduced: "The reduction recently made in the prisoners' ration was for the purpose of bringing it nearer to what the rebel authorities profess to allow their soldiers, and no complaint has been heard of its insufficiency." This is a curious statement given the problems the Confederacy was having feeding its troops and the Union prisoners under its care. If the Confederate soldiers were on a near-starvation diet, then so too would their soldiers in captivity.

Still another reduction in food allocations occurred on September 17, 1864. Col. Hoffman wrote, "Surgeon Thompson recommends a change in some of the articles of the ration. No change can be made except so far as to make it conform to the recent law fixing the ration, which takes off the potatoes and molasses and reduces the hard bread from sixteen to twelve ounces in camp or garrison."

Food was one of the most frequent topics of prisoner diary entries and memoirs. A careful review of the primary sources suggests the diet was varied to a small extent, probably due to the availability of certain foods. Prior to the reductions in the spring and summer of 1864, the men usually received bread/crackers and coffee for breakfast. Sugar was available for coffee, and the prisoners occasionally received bacon and a teaspoon of molasses, but these were rare commodities, especially after the first winter. For dinner, the men usually received some sort of vegetable soup, probably to reduce the incidence of scurvy, pickled pork, salt beef or fresh beef. The men occasionally received potatoes for dinner, at least prior to September, 1864. Prison officials tried to provide fresh beef at least once a week. When possible, the cooks often poured a small amount of vinegar over the meat to help combat scurvy.

The men complained about the quality of the food. Anthony Keiley recalled soup was a half pint of watery slop; not nearly as bad as the "bowl of brackish gruel." Some prisoners complained after the war the food was of inferior quality and often "rancid." The kitchen staff did not help matters—it was prepared by prisoners, who, according to Capt. Clay Dickinson, were poor chefs, as they were "not selected for their cooking qualities."

If the men expected a special meal at Christmas, they were sadly disappointed. Virginian James Payton wrote that for Christmas, 1864, the men received an eighth of a pound (2 oz.) of poor beef and a slice of bread for breakfast; for dinner, a pint of vegetable soup and a piece of bread. Had Payton been in the prison the Christmas before, his meals would have been even more Spartan. North Carolinian, Bartlett Malone on Christmas, 1863 received a piece of bread and a cup of coffee for breakfast and for dinner, a small slice of meat, pint of soup, and five crackers.

While the men craved a more varied diet, they were more concerned about securing enough food to quiet their grumbling stomachs and provide the energy needed to survive. Virginia artilleryman George Neese recalled a daily ration included: "4 ounces of meat, 14 ounces of bread, and 1 pint of bean soup." He admitted "the rations we get are all good in quality, but much too diminutive in quantity; I have been hungry ever since I was captured." Charles Hutt recorded in his diary on Feb. 18: "Our days ration consisted of one small loaf of bread, two ounces of meat and half pint carrot soup. Isn't it shameful!" James Payton on October 29, 1864, received "10 ounces of bread, 1/8 lb [2 oz.] beef or pork, one pint of soup, some salt."

The year before, Bartlett Malone received five crackers and a cup of coffee for breakfast and for dinner a small ration of meat and two crackers, three potatoes and a cup of soup. Some of the men recalled their daily ration was 3 oz. of bread, 2-3 oz of beef or pork, and vegetable soup. Crackers were often substituted for the fresh bread. On December 29, 1864, James Payton recorded the men received nine crackers instead of fresh bread.

South Carolinian, Barry Benson, recalled during his incarceration early in the prison's tenure: "as a whole, I don't think Confederate prisoners suffered greatly for food, tho' we had none too much truly." In a later diary entry (October 31, 1864) James Payton noted, "We have hardly enough to eat and stay hungry all the time." Charles Hutt wrote on February 11, 1864, "Rations we get is not more than half enough." C.W. Jones recalled that "I have seen men eat anything that they can lay their hands on." This included a dead seagull. Dead over a month, it was eaten "with gusto." The men also hunted rats, which they cooked and consumed with relish.

There was never enough food to satisfy the men's cravings. Prisoner James Hall explained there was "nothing that a man can eat. The crackers are as hard as flint stone, and full of worms. I don't believe that God ever intended for one man to pen another up and keep him in this manner. We ought to have enough to eat, anyway." In fairness to the Northern authorities, soldiers in the Union armies commonly complained about these same issues.

The love of all soldiers—coffee—had been provided to the prisoners through June 1, 1864. On that date, Secretary of War, Edwin Stanton issued orders barring the provision of coffee and sugar to all but the sick and wounded as a form of retaliation for the treatment of Union soldiers in Southern prisons. By the end of the month, the army's Chief Surgeon, C.T. Alexander asked the order be rescinded because it appeared it was increasing the number of sick Confederate prisoners. Whether it was because they were truly sick, or used this as an excuse to get their coffee, is not known. Many of the soldiers were not upset by the cessation of their coffee ration because of its poor quality. One private remarked the "commissary actually shook a small bag of coffee at each kettle." Some resorted to other substitutes, such as hot beverages made from burned bread crust.

Because they could no longer provide coffee at breakfast, the prison authorities were forced to change their feeding routine. A prisoner recalled receiving "a piece of bread and meat for breakfast and bean soup (with very few beans) for dinner." He noted sometimes the authorities provided a little variety in the fare but it did not increase in quantity or quality.

To understand what the men experienced in the winter of 1864-65, imagine receiving a fast food restaurant-sized regular hamburger for breakfast and a bowl of watery soup for supper. While the men would not starve on this diet, their caloric intake was severely limited and all but the wealthiest were constantly hungry. According to historian Lonnie Spear, "In effect, then, after late 1864 Confederate soldiers received nearly one-fourth the original established army ration—a mere handful of food—once a day."

Officers were apparently accorded a diet superior in quality and quantity to the enlisted men's. Capt. Clay Dickinson, who was housed at Point Lookout early in its tenure, claimed "the fare at Point Lookout was better than at any other place in which I was confined." During the morning, the officers received chicory coffee and bread and dinner consisted of bread, meat, soup made of beans, and occasionally molasses, rice and vinegar (to prevent scurvy).

For prisoners who had money, sutlers provided a variety of tasty treats that could supplement the men's bland diet (see Chapter 7). Charles Hutt apparently received greenbacks from family and friends back home. He recorded in his diary on July 16. 1864 that he purchased food so his breakfast consisted of ham, eggs, butter, coffee, and biscuits. At times he bought beer, cigar, and pies. He was definitely the exception, as most of the men relied solely on the prison for their meals. As part of retaliation orders, all sutler sales of food and clothing ended on August 10, 1864. Package deliveries to prisoners were also all but eliminated. They could only be provided by "near relatives" and only when the prison was "destitute." Even then, the package delivery had to be approved by the camp commandant.

This did not mean they ate all the meager food they received. Some chose to be even hungrier so they could barter, gamble or buy items from other prisoners. Hearing of this situation, Col. Hoffman issued orders in late fall, 1863 that sutlers could no longer sell food to the prisoners. A further blow was prisoners could no longer receive boxes of goods from friends or family. This continued until early spring, 1864 (March), when the regulations were relaxed, partially because the prison was having difficulty providing adequate food. The ban was reinstated on August 10, 1864,—no sutlers and no packages. Because some prisoners used their food for bartering or gambling was used as justification by the government to further cut rations: "They must have an abundance of food if they can use it for other purposes."

Not only did the men complain of the quality and quantity of their rations—they also worried about being reduced to lowly creatures. When called to the mess hall, the men were not permitted to sit—no chairs were provided, and no utensils graced the tables—they were forced to simply grab the food in front of them and consume it as they left the building.

**Water**

Surrounded by water, one would think the men had plentiful supplies of water, but this was not the case. The water from both the Potomac River and Chesapeake Bay are brackish and unfit for drinking. Prison authorities dug wells during the construction phase. There were as many as six of them, but most yielded tainted water, either with excessive alkaline salts or with iron sulfate, which yellowed clothes and smelled horrible. Only two of the wells were fit for human consumption and one was used for patients in the Hammond Hospital. Dr. Swalm in his U.S. Sanitary Commission report did not comment on the water, as all understood it was a major issue needing to be addressed.

Private Freeman Jones recalled

> *The worse suffering we endured was for water. There were some four or five wells in camp, but in only two cases was the water fit to drink. Of course everyone wanted water from those two wells, and the consequence was they were soon in such a condition that you could not get water from them. The water from the other wells was simply horrid. They had a sweet taste being impregnated with Copperas [iron sulfate], and after standing awhile there was always a deposit on the surface upon which you could write your name. I believe that this water produced more sickness and suffering than any other cause in the prison.*

Anthony Keiley explained, "A scum rises on the top of a vessel if it is left standing during the night, which reflects the prismatic colors as distinctly as the surface of a stagnant pool." He recalled suffering an immediate bout of diarrhea after drinking his first cup.

Despite its poor quality, most men continued to drink from the wells. According to Luther Hopkins, the pumps were "always surrounded by a thirsty crowd of 40–50 prisoners, each with his tin cup, trying to wedge his way in, that he might quench his thirst." Many understood the danger of drinking the water and went without, such as George Neese, who wrote, "The water is not fit to drink, as it produces a diarrhea which sticks closer than a brother, and has already killed hundreds of our prisoners."

Prisoners volunteering for work details were permitted to drink out of a good well near the gate designated for use by the prison guards/personnel. This was an added incentive for volunteering for these often strenuous activities (See Chapter 7).

Report after report on the conditions at Point Lookout cited water as a major concern, but nothing was done to remedy the situation until Quartermaster General Montgomery Meigs got involved in July, 1864. He issued an order: "let two canal-boats be fitted with casks and pumps . . . so as to be filled with fresh water of the Potomac, [and] towed to Point Lookout and moored at the dock." This water would come from the northern reaches of the river where the water is not brackish. A report by Surgeon C.T. Alexander on camp conditions noted the water supplies were "deficient, quality bad."

Despite Meig's intervention, nothing was done until September as additional men fell ill because of tainted water. An investigation showed a miscommunication between the Assistant Quartermaster and the boat captains was the culprit. Finally, beginning in October, 1864, two steamers, *Ide* and *Commodore Foote*, regularly plied the Potomac carrying a total of 40,000 gallons each trip and this continued through the end of the war. Additional wells were dug in October, 1864 and this also helped address the problem. Deaths from diarrhea declined after this point.

Historian James Gillispie believed the Union authorities were directly to blame for the vast majority of prisoner deaths at Point Lookout because they were preventable. "Failing to effectively address the impure water problems at Point Lookout in a timely manner unquestionably increased sickness and mortality figures there and it was unquestionably the Federal officials' fault," he wrote.

## Clothing

The early days of the prison were difficult for the Confederates as policies and procedures were still being developed. One of the most onerous was issued by Col. Hoffman on August 12, 1863 and it would haunt him during the war and after: "You will issue no clothing of any kind except in cases of utmost necessity. So long as a prisoner has clothing upon him, however much torn, you must issue nothing to him, nor must you allow him to receive clothing from any but members of his immediate family, and only when they are in absolute want."

## The U.S. Sanitation Commission Report Concerning Clothing (November, 1863)

Dr. Swalm was perhaps most concerned about the condition of the prisoners' clothing:

> *They [the prisoners] are ragged and dirty and very thinly clad; that is, the very great majority. Occasionally you will find one the fortunate possessor of an overcoat . . . these serve as coverings for the rags beneath. Others, again, are well supplied as regards underclothing, especially those who are from Baltimore, being sent to them by friends. But the great mass are in a pitiable condition, destitute of nearly everything, which, with their filthy condition, makes them really objects of commiseration. Some are without shirts, or what were once shirts are now hanging in shreds from their shoulders. In others the entire back or front will be gone, while again in some you will see a futile attempt at patching. Their clothing is of all kinds and hues--the gray, butternut, the red of our Zouaves and the light and dark blue of our infantry, all in a dilapidated condition.*

Col. Hoffman was forced to take action after the release of the U.S. Sanitation Commission's report. He wrote to Gen. Marston: "from the report it appears that there is a great want of clothing among many of the prisoners." While acknowledging on November 27, 1863, that it was the "desire of the War Department to provide as little clothing for them as possible, it does not wish them to be left in a very destitute condition which this report represents." He reasoned there was "an abundance of inferior clothing on hand" and it would be better to distribute this inadequate clothing than to risk the wrath of subsequent reports. Gen. Marston assured Col. Hoffman that "frequent inspections are made and coats, pants, shirts, shoes, and blankets issued as health and decency require."

Many friends and family were anxious to help their loved-ones by sending packages with clothing and food. Whether it was because the Government was unable to supply enough clothing to the prisoners, or they didn't want to incur the costs, Sec. of War Edwin Stanton relented on November 27, 1863, finally allowing prisoners to receive "clothing or other articles . . . from members of their immediate family." This was a major change in policy, but it continued to bar packages from friends and other family members. Charles Hutt, who hailed from a wealthy family, received a package from home on March 25. He recorded in his diary that day: "Received a package from Washington City: one pair of pants, shoes, hat, two pair of drawers, two shirts, two handkerchiefs, two pair of socks, comb, toothbrush, soap tobacco."

The prison population at this time numbered 13,110 Confederate soldiers and 201 civilian prisoners. The camp's leaders continued requesting additional clothes throughout the remainder of the war—a commodity that was apparently very slow in arriving. This was probably why the authorities continued loosening their policy on packages from home containing clothing.

The inability to provide sufficient clothing to the prisoners plagued the camp's leaders throughout its existence. Whether this was deliberate act or a supply chain issue, the fact remains the prisoners did not receive the clothes they needed. As the winter of 1864-65 approached, the commander of the camp at that time, Major A. G. Brady, continually requested additional clothing for the prisoners.

In one communication he noted many of the men were barefoot because their shoes had given out. He sought: 4,000 shirts, 3,000 pants, 2,500 pairs of shoes, and 1,500 blankets so each man could have one. The pants arrived, but they were blue in color and Brady would not accept them, because of concerns they would aid in escape efforts.

Shipments of clothes arrived from time to time and they were distributed to the prisoners. The diaries of James Payton and Charles Hutt provide a number of entries relating to clothing distribution. Hutt wrote on January 21, 1864, "We went out and drew clothing. I drew flannel shirt, drawers, pair socks and shoes." Ten days later, he recorded in his diary: "We had inspection by our Yankee Sergeant. The object was to see if our tents were clean and if we needed pants." He wrote on February 24, 1864: "The Yankees gave our division pants," probably because of the inspection on January 31. He also noted clothes were distributed on October 2, 1864, and James Payton reported on November 27, 1864: "They gave all the barefooted men a pair of shoes."

Despite these efforts, many prisoners claimed they received few clothes from prison officials. A Virginia cavalryman captured on September 23, 1864, wrote home on March 1, 1865: "My clothing I must confess are in a rather dilapidated condition." All of his clothing came from other prisoners or the kindness of family and friends. Bartlett Malone, who entered diary entries most every day from November, 1863 through March, 1865 mentioned clothing but once. He wrote on September 2, 1864: "And I have not got any shoes." Mississippian David Holt claimed he went without undergarments his whole time in prison.

One source of clothing came from prisoners being released from the camp. Gen. Ben Butler was told by Col. Hoffman on April 27, 1864: "You will direct all surplus clothing in their possession of the character above described to be taken from them on the flag-of-truce boat and returned to Point Lookout for reissue to other prisoners. They should not be permitted to take with them either caps, blankets, shoes, or greatcoats, and I think it would be advisable to take even their coats from them." Did this mean that prisoners being freed from captivity were left almost devoid of clothing?

Word of the destitute condition of the prisoners reached the Confederate government. They proposed sending cotton bales from Mobile, Alabama to the North. After selling the cotton, the proceeds would be used to purchase clothing for Confederate prisoners. This may explain a communication from the Adjutant General's Office to Gen. James Barnes on January 6, 1865, in response to an inspection of the camp at the end of December. It begins by confirming that adequate clothing was an issue: "If the prisoners are suffering for want of necessary clothing, make a requisition for present wants and it will be submitted to the Quartermaster-General." It then notes: "It is hoped that the rebel authorities will be able to procure clothing for their men in our hands at an early day from the proceeds of a cargo of cotton said to have been shipped from Mobile with that object." Depending on the enemy to provide clothing for its soldiers is a highly questionable and irregular approach to caring for prisoners. In fairness to the North, they sent food rations to their prisoners in Southern prisons several times during the war.

Given the communications of high level prison authorities, such as Col. Hoffman, the pleas of prison officials, and the letters and diaries of prisoners, it appears clothing was distributed, but it was often inadequate in quality and quantity.

The root cause of the inadequate clothing has never been adequately explained. Some would argue it was because of retaliation against the South, but others believed supply chain issues played a role, as did the general belief the war would soon be over, so why fund new clothing for prisoners.

**Sanitation**
Sanitation is always an issue when large numbers of humans congregate in small areas. This was certainly the case at Point Lookout and it plagued camp leaders and prisoners throughout the war.

Prison authorities tried to maintain a sanitary environment by layering gravel throughout the prison compound and by digging a series of sanitation ditches that wound around the camp. Tents were within two feet of each other, separated by a shallow sanitary drainage ditch, which ran into the main sanitary ditches. These ditches usually did not drain properly and remained filled with filthy water, usually containing human wastes. A visitor to the camp called the smell "almost unbearable."

High water tables prevented latrines from being built. However, being surrounded by two bodies of water had advantages. Several "sinks" were built over the Potomac River on the west side of the camp. Built at the end of long piers, these latrines did not require holding tanks as the "toilets" were merely holes in wood about 25 feet above river. Men simply squatted down on stilts that looked like railroad ties. Wastes dropped down into the water and were swept away by the tides. A number of men complained about this set-up and would not use them, fouling the camp instead.

The men could use the sinks during the day when access was permitted; however, the gates were locked at night, so each company was assigned a large tub for the men to relieve themselves. By morning, these tubs were very heavy, taking the exertions of four men to carry them out to be emptied into the waterways.

The inadequate numbers of tubs led some anxious men to simply relieve themselves in the streets or sanitary drainage ditches. A report from the U.S. Sanitary Commission in early November, 1863 reported "filth is gradually accumulating and the sinks [night tubs] are not at all thought of, requiring a little extra exertion to walk to them. [Prisoners] void their excrement in the most convenient places to them, regardless of the comfort of others." A subsequent inspection the following month noted the night tubs were insufficient in number and were not promptly emptied in the morning.

The use of clay to make bricks for fireplaces (see below) was a boon to the men, but it also created more misery because the pits created by removing the clay quickly became filled with human excrement as many men preferred to use them rather than the sinks.

The prevalence of human wastes spread diseases, especially dysentery, which is a persistent form of diarrhea. This exacerbated the sanitation issues because bouts of discomfort came on so violently the men could not hold on until they got to a sink.

# The U.S. Sanitation Commission Report Regarding Sanitation (November, 1863)

Dr. Swalm commented on the poor condition of the sinks: "it is a perfect mystery that there is not more sickness than they have, and God knows they have enough, for they live, eat, and sleep in their own filth." He also expressed dissatisfaction with the ditches, which he wrote, "were dug, but they are worse than useless, constantly filled with water, and afford another place to throw filth." He laid the blame for the filth and other sanitary issues squarely on the prison authorities, writing, "It is our fault when the officer in command fails to place in charge some one of good executive ability, capable of giving commands and seeing that they are enforced, one who will have the camp regularly policed and severely punish any offender of the sanitary rules." He urged the prison authorities to "give employment to a certain number of men every day" who could work to improve the camps' sanitation.

Gen. Marston was outraged by the section of the report dealing with inadequate sanitation. In response, he wrote: "the camp is policed every day. The drainage is not good, and will not be until some genius equally as brilliant as the author of this report in question discovers a method of causing water to flow as readily from a level surface not much elevated above the surrounding seas." He also took issue with the implication that the men were dirty because of his negligence: "That they are a dirty, lousy set is true enough, but having afforded them every facility for cleanliness the duty of the Government in this regard as respects the well men is accomplished."

## Tents

Point Lookout was the *only* Federal prison not housing prisoners in barracks-type buildings. Finding enough tents to house the ever-increasing prison population posed major problems for prison authorities. Gen. Marston reported in October, 1863, the camp was composed of 810 tents to house the 7,600 men (an average of 9.3 men per tent). The vast majority, 720, was "common" tents and the rest were a hodge-podge of various types. On November 9, 1863, an additional 1,800 prisoners arrived at Point Lookout, enlarging the population to more than 9,000 men. Tents were slow in arriving, so the prisoners suffered. A report issued on December 17, 1863, reported the camp contained 980 tents or 170 more than in October. Many tents were of an inferior quality, but this concerned the camp authorities less than finding enough of them. The number and quality of tents continued to be problematic throughout the war. A communication from the Quartermaster's Department on May 24, 1864, is telling: "The Quartermaster's Department will decide which kind [of tents] can best be spared. Old tents, or even shanties, will answer all purposes for prisoners."

## The U.S. Sanitation Commission Report Regarding Tents (Nov., 1863)

According to Dr. Swalm, tents appeared to be in fairly good condition during the early stages of the war. "Of their shelter there can be no possible complaint, for they all have good tents, such as wall, hospital, Sibley, wedge, shelter, hospital, and wall-tent flies. Majority are in the wedge tent. Average in a hospital tent, from 15 to 18 men; in wall tent, from 10 to 12; in shelter tent, 3; in Sibley tent, from 13 to 14; in wedge tent, 5; under hospital fly tent, 10 to 13; under wall-tent fly, from 3 to 8." He was concerned about the living conditions inside the tents noting they were "in keeping with the inmates, filthy; pieces of cracker, meat, ashes, &c., strewn around the tent, and in which they will lie."

The Union high command did not have taken issue with Dr. Swalm's rosy report, but prisoners and some camp officials did, especially as the war dragged on. The camp's commander during the latter phases of its operation, Maj. A.G. Brady, complained in October, 1864, that fully a third of the tents in the camp were unfit for use.

Some prisoners claimed the prison became so crowded they never saw the inside of a tent and were forced to lie on the cold ground with little protection. A former Virginia artilleryman recalled, "I slept on the damp sand for two months without any sign of a blanket or bedding under me, and nothing but my shoe for a pillow." A Mississippian had a different experience in his tent: "I was given a bunk made out of the tops of cracker boxes and about two feet wide. As the weather was warm, I doubled my blanket under me to soften the cracker box tops. I had no cover and never pulled off my clothes except when I went in swimming or washed my shirt. Underwear I did not possess."

William Haigh arrived at the camp on January 22, 1865. He recalled: "we were put into an old rickety tent without a fire or fuel to pass the night on the damp ground, with no covering but a blanket and nothing to protect us from the ground." Many men commented on the wet ground in the tents, which created an unhealthy environment. Haigh noted the ground "retains water, becomes slushy and slippery and at all times [is] damp inside the tents." Rainy conditions were especially difficult for the men, as the tents often leaked. B.T. Holliday recalled when it rained, "we spent a very uncomfortable time."

So many men in tents did not make for optimal sleeping arrangements. The body-to-body arrangement was a problem in the summer because of the intense heat, causing many to get too much of it. It worked better in the winter, for despite little firewood, few blankets, and rags for clothes, the men found a measure of comfort by sharing each other's body heat. "Spooning" was deployed during the cold months, even when men were not crammed into the tents. They formed circles within the tent, with one man behind and another in front. A prisoner recalled that "when we wanted to turn over in the night, the signal was given to turn, and all made the turn from necessity." The close quarters led to the spread of disease, vermin, and constant bickering.

Officers initially housed at Point Lookout appeared to have access to better accommodations. Capt. Henry Dickinson recalled "We were quartered in large Sibley tents, which were quite comfortable." A reporter for the *New York Herald* wrote "their tents are floored and furnished with stoves, and they are allowed three meals per day."

The men secured cracker boxes to make floors. The cracker boxes were made of sturdy white pine and measured 32 inches long, 20 inches wide, and 12 inches deep. After their contents were removed/used, the boxes went to the commissary where they could be purchased by the prisoners for 10 to 15 cents apiece. Some of the boxes were used for tent flooring, with sides that rose up the side for a foot to keep the occupants of the tent dry. Charles Hutt recorded in his diary, "We have to raise our tents on cracker boxes which greatly add to our comfort."

Men of greater means were able to construct entire houses from these cracker boxes. Bartlett Malone and five other prisoners pooled their resources and built a house in 1864 costing $8.80 for materials and another $8.00 for a stove from the camp sutler. As a point of reference, a full month's pay for an enlisted man in the Union army was $12. These houses were placed in one row, constituting a division. Some were large enough to accommodate as many as a dozen men. A *New York Herald* reporter believed that the "aristocratic and wealthy," occupied these houses. They were marked with such names as "Virginia Hall," "Eldon Hall" and "The Rebel Retreat."

The poor quality of the tents continued plaguing the prisoners and prison officials until the end of the war. The Adjutant General's Office wrote to Gen. Barnes in response to an inspection the end of December, 1864: "if in your opinion a portion of the tents are unfit for further use you will cause them to be inspected in the usual manner and submit the report to this office, with such suggestions as you may deem proper to make." Barnes apparently made this request many times without receiving the tents he requested.

## Keeping Warm

Winter nights at Point Lookout often hovered between zero and freezing and the canvas tents did little to keep out the cold. Many of the men spoke of their personal challenges in keeping warm. That is, however, a relative term, affected by adequacy of clothing, tents, fireplaces/firewood, and blankets. It was in this arena that the U. S. Sanitation Commission report had the most impact.

Winter flooding added to the prisoners' misery. According to A. M. Keiley, "a high tide and an easterly gale would flood the whole surface of the pen, *and freeze as it flooded,* the sufferings of the half-clad wretches, many accustomed to the almost vernal warmth of the Gulf, may easily be imagined. Many died outright, and many more will go to their graves crippled and racked with rheumatisms, which they date from the winter of 1863-4."

## The U.S. Sanitation Commission Report on Warmth (November, 1863)

Dr. Swalm noted ". . . almost every tent throughout the camp has fireplace and chimney built of brick made by them from the soil (which is clay) and sun baked. In a few of the Sibleys holes are dug, fire built, and covered at the top. Generally the tents are filled with smoke." Swalm went on to explain that wood was an issue: "Although they have fireplaces, wood is not issued to them, but they are allowed to go out in squads every day and gather such as may be found in the woods where trees have been cut down, but they are not allowed to cut down others." Therefore, it is clear that adequate firewood was a concern at the onset of the first winter. Inadequate blankets were also a concern. Swalm continued: ". . . they are poorly supplied with blankets [so] they must have suffered severely from the cold, more so where they are, for it is a very bleak place. On visiting the quarters, found them crowded around a few coals in their respective tents, some having good blankets thrown across the shoulders, others pieces of carpet, others a gum blanket, others a piece of oilcloth commonly used for the covering of the tables. Generally they have one blanket to three men, but a great many are entirely without."

Gen. Marston bitterly complained about this part of the report, writing that each prisoner was issued a blanket, "unless he has sold or gambled it away." He admitted that shortages occurred from time to time upon, "the arrival of a large number of prisoners without blankets the quartermaster has not had enough to supply them, but it is not so now." Buried in a note to Gen. Marston from Col. Hoffman later in the war (March 30, 1864) is a very telling sentence: "as there is now a large quantity of inferior blankets on hand, only suitable to issue to prisoners, it is not advisable or economical to purchase others." Why blankets unacceptable for Union soldiers were fine for Confederate prisoners was not explained.

The response to the U.S. Sanitation Commission's report was swift, leading to each man receiving one blanket as winter approached. But one blanket provided little protection, and inspections (see below) sought to confiscate additional blankets. The blankets were often of poor quality and unusable. During an inspection on Nov. 6, 1864, James Payton reported, "They gave out blankets, but ours were all damaged by seawater and some had holes in the center."

It was during these periods the men's inadequate clothing created the most problems. James Payton noted in his diary on November 13, 1864: "Today, it is very cold and windy. The wind comes off the water and goes clean through you. I have no overcoat."

The men realized clay soil in part of the camp could be used to make bricks to build fireplaces in their tents. Some entrepreneurs went into business making bricks and selling them for three cents apiece. One inspection indicated, "Nearly all of the tents are provided with fireplaces and chimneys built of bricks manufactured by the prisoners." The fireplaces required a constant supply of wood, but that was not always forthcoming.

Firewood was a scarce commodity as the prison pens were devoid of vegetation. Wood was distributed from mid-November through February, but did not help with cold nights in October and March. The amounts distributed were also inadequate: Each division (1,000 men) received a cord of wood each day. If a cord contains 500 - 600 pieces of wood, it meant the men did not receive a piece every day. Indeed, Charles Hutt recorded in his diary on February 3, 1864: "we have not the first stick of wood for it is our day to miss," suggesting men probably received wood every other day, which would explain how a cord of wood could be allocated to a thousand men. This would mean a Sibley tent with say 14 men would receive seven pieces of wood all day—hardly enough to keep the men warm for 24-hours.

The wood the men received was often of poor quality. Artilleryman George Neese described it as green pine "which never fails to make more smoke than fire." Neese continued that the wood "allowed each tent was not enough to keep a little fire more than a day in a week, and actually I have not seen nor felt a good fire this whole winter." Several prisoners agreed, commenting in their diaries they went fully eight days without wood during the exceptionally cold winter of 1864-65. North Carolinian Bartlett Malone noted when wood was provided it was, "one shoulder turn of pine bush every other day."

Prisoner Alfred Smith wrote in his diary for October 30, 1864, (before firewood was distributed), "No wood allowed to make fires. All shiver for want of clothes, blankets and rations, suffering are general and keen." The lack of this commodity, more than any other caused a general feeling among the prisoners that "Yankees don't care if we freeze," and apparently some did die during the harsh winters. What made matters worse was although each man had a blanket and could "spoon" with others to keep warm, there was nothing the men could place under them to protect them from the frigid ground.

During particularly cold and windy days without firewood, the men almost froze. A Virginian explained how the men could survive a cold snap during November, 1864: "We ran around the camp to try and warm up." James Payton inscribed in his diary on November 2, 1864: "I nearly froze sitting in the house as we have no way to make a fire. My feet felt like lumps of ice. I went to the bulletin board and ran around a good deal trying to keep warm." The year before a prisoner recorded in his diary as the snow fell, not one stick of wood could be found in the camp. The men resorted to marching in place in their tents.

Nights were the biggest problem as the men were not permitted to roam around the camp, seeking to get warm. As seen earlier, the men often spooned and shared blankets to get through the cold spells. At least one man froze to death when another prisoner would not share his blanket, and James Payton recorded in his diary on December 12, 1864, two men froze to death during the night and Bartlett Malone reported five froze to death on January 1, 1864.

Those who went out on work details were often fortunate enough to return with bundles of wood. James Payton recorded in his diary on November 17, 1864: "The men on detail generally pick up enough coal and wood to keep them warm. Those who do not go on detail must freeze." They also sold bundles of wood for "30 cents a load." Payton disparaged this as "it is green pine, though."

A modern-day historian studying the historical record noted wood was never to be restricted under Union retaliation orders, but availability was an issue at Point Lookout. Much of the problem arose from the scarcity of wood near

Point Lookout and what was available, was of poor quality. During the early days of camp life, much of the wood came from a stand of pine located near the camp.

## Inspections

Men were inspected every Sunday. Other spot inspections occurred without warning. The men lined up and stock was taken of their condition. Additional clothes and shoes were often distributed during these periods. While the men were out of their tents, prison guards roamed through the camp looking for excess blankets, escape implements, and anything else considered contraband. During one inspection the guards actually found a boat being constructed for escape purposes. The men were very creative in hiding materials, in some instances under floorboards.

## The Camp Hospital

As previously described, the camp hospital became an important component of the prisoners' well-being. Most never saw the inside of Hammond General Hospital because their illnesses were not serious enough to warrant it. Most did, however, visit the camp hospital for treatment of a variety of illnesses. The hospital was described in 1863 as being "situated in the southern part of the encampment and was composed of eighteen hospital tents, complete, arranged two together, end to end, and placed in two rows, a broad street intervening, with the cook and dining tent on the eastern end and facing the street."

As one can imagine, when Dr. Swalm of the U.S. Sanitary Commission came to visit the prison, his first evaluation was of the camp hospital. He began his analysis by writing: "The accommodations here were much better than I expected to find them and much more comfortable, yet they had by no means the best of care." Despite this initial statement, Gen. Marston's was furious with the report, believing a number of statements were erroneous.

## Living Arrangements in the Hospital Pen

Dr. Swalm found "In these tents there were 100 patients, and all, with the exception of five or six, were on raised bunks, and all were lying on mattresses with at least one blanket for covering." He observed, however, "there being no stoves in the hospital, the men complain greatly of cold, and I must admit that for the poor emaciated creatures suffering from diarrhea one single blanket is not sufficient." Gen. Marston complained the report was inaccurate, claiming each bed contained two blankets.

## Types of Illnesses Treated in the Hospital Pen

"Chronic diarrhea is the most prevalent disease, yet they have mild cases of remittent fever and some erysipelas," Dr. Swalm found. "Mortality, none, for when any cases assume a dangerous character they are immediately removed to the general hospital, and they generally remove from twenty to thirty per day on an average, leaving in camp hospital eighty sick." He was especially concerned that patients were not grouped by illness: "Wounded and erysipelas (a severe skin disease causing skin rashes accompanied by fever and vomiting caused by a streptococcal bacterium), fever and diarrhea, were lying side by side." He noted with satisfaction more serious cases were immediately sent to Hammond General Hospital for more professional treatment.

## Hospital Pen Personnel

Dr. Swalm found the hospital not staffed by Union personnel. "Eight of their own men were detailed to take care of them, and although they were enlisted men, yet six were graduates from some medical school and the other two had been students." This could work, he believed, if the prisoners detailed to this duty cared about their patients. He noted, however, that "little or no attention did they give to their sick comrades, and, except in giving the necessary food and medicine, they scarcely even visited them. There is either a lack of sympathy or else indolence enters largely into their composition, and I am inclined to believe it is the latter, for, with the accommodations at their command, with good beds and shelter for the sick, if they had one particle of pride they could render them much more comfortable, especially as regards cleanliness."

General Marston complained about this portion of the report, explaining "two or three nurses are assigned to every ward, one of whom is always present therein day and night." He felt the patients were not being neglected in any way.

## Hospital Pen Sanitation
The physical appearance of the patients disturbed Dr. Swalm: "they are in a filthy condition; faces and hands apparently strangers to soap and water and hair seemingly uncombed for weeks." Gen. Marston took issue with this statement, "There is a laundry for cleansing the clothing of sick men and the hospital is abundantly supplied with washbasins, towels, and soap."

## Medicine Availability in the Hospital Pen
Dr. Swalm noted the "dispensary is a poor apology for one, having little or nothing but a few empty bottles. Not a particle of oil or salts, in fact, a cathartic of no kind. About half a dram of opium, half pound of sulphether, half pound of simple cerate, and a few other things constitute the whole supply." He was also concerned about a lack of cleanliness and orderliness of the medications: "everything covered with dust and what few articles they had were exposed to the air and placed indiscriminately along the counter and in the most perfect confusion; were going to arrange the bottles, &c." Gen. Marston admitted that "at one time there was considerable delay in filling the surgeon's requisition for medicines, but during that period he was furnished with medicines from the general hospital."

## Hospital Pen Food
"The rations are very good, both in quantity and quality; amply sufficient for any sick man; but there are exceptional cases where they need something more delicate than the regular army ration," noted Dr. Swalm. The patients regularly received beef/pork, potatoes, coffee/tea, rice, molasses, and hardtack crackers. Soup and soft bread was provided about once a week. No utensils were provided, so the patients were forced to eat with their hands, similar to the general prison population.

## Fixing the Problems of the Hospital Prison Pen
Dr. Swalm believed "a great amount of the misery experienced in the hospital and throughout the camp might be obviated if a little more energy

was displayed by the surgeon in charge [Dr. Bunton of the 2nd New Hampshire Infantry] . . . The assistants saw what was needed and were determined to entirely renovate and change the whole condition and aspect. If done, much suffering might be alleviated add less sickness would ensue."

Fence, deadline, and gate to beach
John Jacob Omenhausser sketchbook, 1864-1865, Maryland Manuscripts Collection, #5213, Special Collections, University of Maryland Libraries

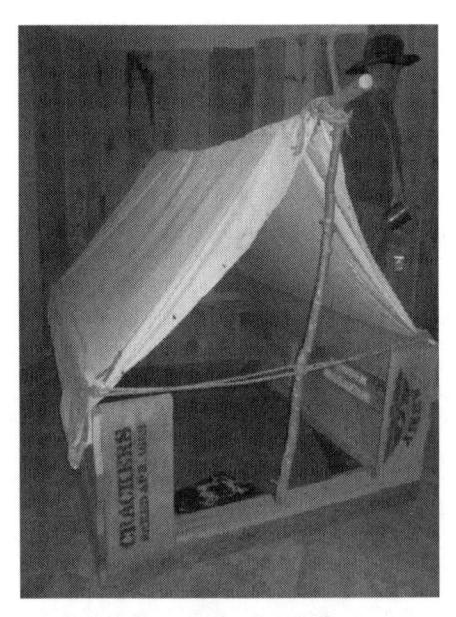

Replica of tent with floor and sides lined with cracker boxes at Point Lookout State Park

# Chapter 7
## Passing the Time

Men incarcerated at Point Lookout had little hope for the future. Unlike non-military prison sentences, there is no "release time" provided. Men remained until they were exchanged, paroled, the war ended, they died, or in rare incidents, they escaped. The time spent in the Point Lookout prison camp was very stressful and some never recovered from their stay in Southern Maryland. Much of the stress arose from uncertainty: Uncertainty about their future, of the well-being of their families and their comrades in arms. They worried about illness and whether they would ever see the outside of the prison. Interactions with prison guards were also sources of stress. Then there was the monotony. Anthony Keiley wrote the prison had "all the stupidity of a treadmill without the exercise."

Some men just gave up hope and sank into a deep depression. A Virginian described that one of his tent-mates who had been in the prison for over a year had "given up all hopes of ever being paroled, and had become disconsolate, ragged, dirty and shiftless, his clothes tattered and torn from long service without change." Charles Nutt recorded in his diary on April 29, 1864: "I am exceedingly low spirited and cannot hear anything to dispel the dark cloud of despair which hangs over me."

George Neese wrote, "The true aspects . . . of prison life in general can never be described [so no one can understand] . . . the melancholy gloom that settles down like the eternal night on the spirit of the man and crushes hope to the dark recesses of its lowest stage, so that life itself becomes a burden that may be dragged, but too wearisome to bear. No painter's palette ever held the color black enough to truthfully delineate the shows that constantly hang around a prisoner of war in these United States." He went on to explain that "I have not seen one man's smile or heard a hearty laugh since I've been here. Everyone moves around in almost sullen silence, with a sad countenance, and the whole crew looks as if they had just returned from a big funeral."

It did not help so many of their comrades were sick and dying. John King recalled the "poor fellows died rapidly, despondent, homesick, hungry and wretched. I have stood day after day watching the wagons carry the dead outside to be buried and each day for several weeks 16 dead men were taken through the gate."

**Routine**
Every day was like the one before, so men sought ways to pass the time.
It took less than a month in the camp for Hiram Williams to feel the despair. "The prison life is getting unendurable," he wrote on April 26, 1865. "The weary monotony of day after day, is awful . . . I dread the coming of each day."

Mississippian David Holt recalled a typical day: "We answered roll-call every morning and evening. The remainder of the time we roamed around hunting for something to do or see." The men headed to the mess halls at 8:00 a.m. for breakfast and again between 2 – 3 p.m. for dinner. They did not receive "supper."

After breakfast, the men spent some time sweeping the streets and cleaning up trash, supervised by one of Southern sergeants. The rest of the day was unstructured, and the men struggled to get through another day, equally wretched as the day before.

The day ended with taps, sounded at about 9:00 p.m. Because the men were concerned that guards would shoot into a tent if they heard noises, Point Lookout "was nearly as quiet as a cemetery" after taps, according to a prisoner. Guards roamed through camps and could shoot anyone who was out of his tent. The prisoners reported the guards carried six-shooter pistols—easier to use against a prisoner after dark.

Even Christmas was like any other day. James Payton wrote in his diary, "Christmas: "A dismal and sorrowful Christmas, but we still have many things to be thankful for. We are still living and the Lord has not called us to judgment for our sins."

## Packages/Letters from Home

The men could receive and send letters. Any money received was removed and given to the sutler in the prisoner's name. Outgoing letters were stamped: "Prisoner's letter examined and approved." Each could only be one sheet in length and was read by the commandant or another authority before leaving the prison. Any passages dealing with the adverse conditions of the camp were censored before being mailed. The men were able to get around space limitations by writing in exceptionally small print.

Marcus Toney saved two days' rations and traded them for five cents, which he used to purchase one sheet of paper, one envelope, and one stamp. He sent the letter to a friend in Baltimore, who sent additional clothes and a ten pound container of tobacco which he used to barter.

Packages from home were periodically restricted by prison authorities. Despite a scurvy outbreak in November, 1863, Col. Hoffman reiterated his opposition to packages from home: "I do not think it well to permit them to receive boxes of eatables from their friends, and I suggest you have them informed that such articles will not hereafter be delivered. I have granted some permission for these things, but hereafter I will say it is against orders."

Boxes of food and clothing were prohibited for several reasons. Bickering and fights often occurred when some prisoners received boxes and others did not. Restricting of boxes also became a component of Sec. of War Edwin Stanton's retaliation campaign to punish the prisoners for the conditions in Southern prisoner of war camps.

Hoffman reissued this prohibition on February 15, 1864, stating to camp officials, "permit no article of food to be delivered to them." He used the rationale that the "Government furnishes them with an abundance to eat, and the delivery of boxes of eatables from their friends is attended with much inconvenience to commanders, creates dissatisfaction among those who receive nothing, and gives opportunity for sympathizers to show their interest in rebels."

Restrictions on clothing were relaxed somewhat by the end of November, 1863 with the onset of winter and the prisoners having insufficient clothing to weather it. The clothes could only come from "members of their immediate family," however. This was further relaxed later in the winter and spring when the prison authorities realized they were unable or unwilling to provide for the prisoners' food and clothing needs.

District Commander Gen. Ben Butler, was a strong proponent of the prisoners' receiving any and all boxes from home. He wrote to Col. Hoffman on February 20, 1864, "I agree fully that the delivery of packages to prisoners causes the commanders of camps a great deal of trouble. The question certainly gives me a great deal, but I undergo that trouble very cheerfully, and would if it were twice as much, in order that our prisoners may get even small alleviations for their sufferings than that which they receive from their friends." This was a remarkable confession from a senior officer. He continued, "I have conversed with many of our prisoners on that subject and they say that the boxes received from their friends have been almost a source of support to them . . ."

Butler also explained the Confederacy was allowing Union prisoners to receive boxes. "I cannot ask the Confederate commissioner to deliver boxes to our prisoners from their friends while I refuse to deliver boxes from their friends to their prisoners." He felt it was a punishment to withhold the boxes—an act that could occur due to the wrong doing of a prisoner. To everyone's relief, the War Department accepted Butler's request on March 2, 1864 and the boxes flowed to the prisoners once again

## The Beach

The three prison gates leading to the Chesapeake Bay were opened every day in good weather and men could spend considerable time on its beach.
A fourth gate also opened to the Chesapeake, but it was further north, near the guards' headquarters, and was used for transporting materials into camp after being unloaded from ships.

The men spent endless hours enjoying the beach and water. The historian of the 4th Rhode Island Infantry believed the incidence of sickness was reduced because the men could wash their clothes and bodies in the Bay. One prisoner reported washing his soiled clothes and then remained in the water up to his neck while they dried so he would not get sunburned. The men were permitted to keep and eat any crabs or fish they caught. One prisoner recalled it was not unusual for half the prisoners, "eight or ten thousand at a time" disporting in the water, imitating the antics almost of every aquatic animal."

Some enterprising watermen set up shop along the beach, selling their wares to the prisoners. They also offered, for a price, to boil the prisoners' clothing to remove the lice while their owners bathed in the Bay to rid their bodies of the ornery critters. This was but a temporary reprieve, for another batch of lice was waiting for them when they returned to their tents.

The availability of the beach and water may sound somewhat ideal, but it could be deadly. The wastes from the camp drained into the Chesapeake Bay close to these beaches, thus fouling them and the wildlife the men caught. This led to many becoming ill.

The guards were always concerned about escape attempts so they established a "deadline." Demarked by logs driven into the beach and into the water, anyone moving beyond it was in danger of being shot. There were other hazards the men dealt with, such as sea nettles (jellyfish), with stinging tentacles, adding to their misery.

## Personal Hygiene

The prisoners' level of personal hygiene varied. Because of their free access to the Chesapeake Bay in good weather, many bathed and washed their clothes regularly. Soap was apparently available to the prisoners for on October 29, 1864, James Payton wrote, "being salt water, all the soap stuck to my skin." Cold weather ended these activities.

Some men lost all hope and did little but lie on their beds, never washing their bodies or clothes. Many observers noted terrible smells emanated from the prison, not only from human wastes, but also from unwashed bodies.

## Work Details

A number of activities required work details because not enough soldiers or civilians were available to perform these tasks. These included unloading ships carrying supplies, repairing roads, constructing wharves, collecting wood and whitewashing buildings. The historian of the 4th Rhode Island Infantry recalled the details consisted of 50 to 100 men.

A reporter for the *New York Herald* observed *"to get on them [a work detail] is no easy matter, being so much in demand that many a poor fellow has often to exercise his wits and his patience to get the privilege of working a day for a plug of tobacco, a piece of meat and an armful of wood."* A prisoner recalled *"when a requisition was made for a certain number of men to go outside, a thousand would rush for the gate, all eager to get extra rations for their work."*

Some activities, such as unloading ships were most sought after for a number of reasons, including: breaking the monotony of camp life, providing a good form of exercise, and the prospect of being rewarded with additional food or delicacies, such as whisky or sugar. Each man on a work detail cost the Government about $.09 per day. Men also grabbed whatever supplies they could fit into their blouses or pockets. Prisoners on work details also gained access to sailors who provided a wealth of information about what was going on outside the gates. The camps were rife with rumors, usually incorrect, so the men craved accurate information about the war. It was not unusual for a newspaper or two to be given to the prisoners during the offloading process.

Demand to be included in work details far exceeded the ability of the camp to involve all prisoners who requested it. Prison authorities came up with an ingenious way to "encourage" prisoners to pledge their allegiance to the United States. On May 29, 1864, Col. Hoffman ordered camp officials to select men for "fatigue duties" by giving "preference [to those] who avow loyal sentiments and who have applied to take the oath of allegiance."

## Reading

Literate prisoners spent considerable time reading a variety of books and magazines. A lending library was established to circulate materials. It occupied a tent with rough shelves for a minuscule number of volumes. James Payton recalled attempting to visit the library but it was just too crowded. There is no evidence the prison authorities did anything to encourage or discourage its use.

A school was also established. One of the first things Malachi Bowden did upon his incarceration in October, 1864 was to enroll in the school. A prisoner, a "Professor Morgan," who taught at the College of William and Mary prior to the war opened the school on March 15, 1864. Bowden thought Brown was a Methodist minister. Nearly 1,200 were taking classes by July, 1864. The numbers must have dwindled by October, for Brown recalled, "Compared with the large number of prisoners, there were but a few in attendance."

## Gambling

Gambling often becomes a common way to pass the time when men are together and Point Lookout prisoners were no exception. Faro and other card games were most commonly played, as were lotto and dice games. Gambling was not a problem when it was for fun, but when goods and money were involved, trouble followed. "Some persons will go without eating at times to gamble off their crackers," wrote a soldier. Such was the power of the addiction for some men. Authorities would use these occurrences to justify the reduction in food provided to the prisoners in 1864—why would they be bartering rations if they were inadequate to begin with? However, the lure of the game overwhelmed common sense and a prisoner's well-being.

One enterprising prisoner built a gambling den out of cracker boxes. Gambling usually began in the morning and continued all through the day until curfew. Money, tobacco, and crackers were the most common stakes.

A reporter from the *New York Herald* reported "Keno" was the most popular form of gambling. "In this the players, who are provided with cards containing printed numbers and pebbles or buttons, sit down on the ground and await the movements of a dirty, ill-looking fellow, who draws, from a haversack slung at his side, small bits of wood or bone, and calls the numbers on them. In a few minutes a player will say 'keno,' when all eyes look up, the stake being won. Crackers and chews of tobacco comprise the stakes."

Prisoners in other camps throughout the North and South played baseball. This did not occur at Point Lookout, perhaps because the pen was too small to allow a field to be laid out.

**Getting News**
The lack of accurate information of what was going on outside the gates created considerable stress among the men. The rumor mill was a well-oiled machine, only increasing the men's anxiety. As seen earlier, contact with sailors or guards helped the prisoners secure more accurate information.

Rumors were a major problem, as most were inaccurate. The saddest related to the men's incarceration. James Payton noted, "Just for fun, every now and then someone starts a report that the Yankees are going to exchange prisoners. This excites the men and helps their spirits until they find it a hoax." Bulletin boards were used within the camp to convey important information. These included: information on new rules and regulations, offers of pardon to those taking oath of alliance, items lost or found, items for sale, and alerts that letters/packages had arrived.

Prison authorities were also interested in gathering information, but this was about the prisoners. Whenever possible, they identified informants who could provide information about escape attempts or other infractions. This information was exchanged for additional rations.

## Artistic Pursuits

Humans are creative creatures and many men passed the time in theatrical, music, and debate activities. Mess group 22 undertook a debate during a cold winter night. The question was "whether monarch or republicanism was the best form of government." Theatrical troops were also common in these camps as men sought ways to relieve the boredom. One prisoner recalled "A couple of violans [sic], an old banjo, and a tambourine, together with a corps of singers produced an evening's entertainment." During the latter part of November, the "Aeolian Glee Club" was formed.

Some musical groups became quite proficient and performances were given in the mess halls. Charles Hutt paid 15 cents to see a performance on December 1, 1864. Bartlett Malone attended a concert two days later, but only paid ten cents. James Payton headed over to the cookhouse on December 1. He explained, "They have concerts three times a week. I do not go because they charge for coming and I have not money to pay them." Another prisoner recalled much time was spent "singing, wrestling and comic performances."

## Making Items

A number of men used their talents to manufacture items other prisoners found useful. Among the items produced were rings, fans, art works, and clocks. Barter was the currency of exchange. Another benefit accrued by these craftsmen was psychological in nature. The hours spent on creativity helped make the long monotonous days pass much faster.

Some industrious prisoners were able to use old/cast off materials to build engines that could be used for carpentry projects. The historian of the 4th Rhode Island Infantry marveled at the quality of the items as prisoners were not permitted to have hammers, knives, etc. and it turned out their best customers were the prison guards who "bought them to send home as souvenirs of the war."

## Negative Interactions Between Prisoners

Problems commonly occur when men are kept in close quarters, such as Point Lookout. It was not unusual for fights to break out among the men for a variety of reasons. Thievery from tents was also a problem. In some cases, prisoners entered a tent on the pretext of visiting a person, but were really scouting its contents. They returned later, making a slit in the tent wall to remove the items they coveted.

Courts did not exist in the prison, but well-defined ways prisoners punished their own for serious infractions developed, and they could be very harsh. The worst form of punishment involved dipping the head and shoulders of perpetrators in one of the tubs filled with human wastes. A prisoner recalled it was "a terrible punishment—almost equal to being lynched." Realizing the severity of this punishment, the guards tried to intervene whenever they could.

**Getting Needed Supplies**
Sutlers commonly set up shop near most armies, selling a variety of food, personal items, and clothing. When in the field, they would operate as a mobile store, usually selling goods at a premium. The sutlers at Point Lookout often marked up goods 8–10 times higher what would be paid outside the gates. James Payton wrote on December 2, 1864, "They gouge you on everything." Most men avoided using them unless no other way of securing certain goods existed. Others just did not have the cash to pay for items they craved. The Government sanctioned the activities of each sutler, and in return a tax was collected on each item sold. This revenue went into the Prison Fund, which was supposed to benefit the prisoners.

Items sent through the mail were another way prisoners could secure needed goods. As seen earlier, prison authorities opened each piece of mail arriving from the outside and any money they contained were added to the prisoners' sutler accounts. While this worked well if you had money, most of the prisoners never did, or went long stretches without. Therefore, most relied on bartering and trading to get the goods they desired.

Two forms of "currency" were regularly used for bartering. Hardtack crackers, issued with most meals, except when fresh bread was available, were an easy way to pay for goods. Although men found the number crackers issued to be insufficient to their basic needs, some commonly put them in their pockets and used them to barter. Tobacco was a second form of currency. A pound of tobacco was worth one greenback. It could be cut into twenty thumbnail sized portions called "chews" or "quids," which were worth 5 cents each. Generally, one cracker equaled one "chew."

Some men traded services for goods. Some of the trades found in camp were: barbers, dentists, "doctors," shoemakers, tailors, fan-makers, and launderers. A creative prisoner advertised he could remove the stains from teeth from drinking the vile water. Jewelry-making was common pursuit. Joseph Kern noted, "The jewelry shops are without number and all do a good business. They traded in rings, necklaces, and fans.

## Spirituality

Many men were religious when they arrived at Point Lookout and a high number of others eventually sought God as a way of reducing their misery. There were just too few clergymen to minister to the men. Several from St. Mary's County volunteered to visit the camp and hold religious services. Gen. Marston asked Col. Hoffman in early October, 1863 whether he could grant their requests. Hoffman replied, "There is no objection to the visits of clergymen to the prisoners at stated times, provided the prisoners have no objections to such visits. There must, of course, be no doubt about the unqualified loyalty of the clergymen admitted, and their visits must be for religious purposes only, and not to engage in political discussions."

The 4th Rhode Island Infantry historian recalled, "Upon every pleasant evening they [the prisoners] would gather in crowds at different parts of the pen and hold religious services." The services were held in the mess halls during the winter months, but because no fires were lit, the buildings and the men were very cold, discouraging some from attending these services.

## Visitors

Visitors were discouraged. Passes were occasionally provided during the camp's early period, but that changed on May 26, 1864 when Col. Hoffman informed the camp authorities: "Give no more passes to visit prisoners except in case of illness." This order hardened less than two weeks later, when he decreed no visitors would be permitted except by his permission or that of the War Department. In October of 1864, Sec. of War Stanton finally took matters into his own hands, informing prison leadership *only he* could grant permission for visitors.

Many men gambled to pass the time and alleviate boredom
John Jacob Omenhausser sketchbook, 1864-1865, Maryland Manuscripts Collection, #5213, Special Collections, University of Maryland Libraries

One of the trades at Point Lookout: Barber
John Jacob Omenhausser sketchbook, 1864-1865, Maryland Manuscripts Collection, #5213,
Special Collections, University of Maryland Libraries

# Chapter 8
## Guarding the Prisoners

Point Lookout came into existence with a commander, Brigadier General Gilman Marston, but no troops. Marston received orders on July 23, 1863, to "proceed to the Army of the Potomac and report to General Meade for a guard of about 300 men for the prison camp to be established at Point Lookout." Casting about for appropriate troops to detach, Meade settled on the battle weary 2nd, 5th, and 12th New Hampshire Volunteers. These troops began arriving on July 30, 1863 aboard steamers. The 2nd and 12th New Hampshire established their camps along the Potomac River to the west of the prison pens; the 5th New Hampshire pitched tents along the Chesapeake Bay, just north of the stockade. Men of the latter regiment named their quarters, "Camp Cross," to honor their fallen leader, Col. Edward Cross, who was killed at Gettysburg. The men did not have long to wait for their guarding responsibilities to begin, for a steamer soon arrived carrying more than a hundred Confederate prisoners.

After establishing camps, the men's attention turned to their own personal hygiene and they could be seen bathing in the Potomac River and washing their filthy clothes. They received new uniforms on August 1, 1863 and threw away their old worn-out garments. With little to do but guard a handful of prisoners, the men believed they had drawn the best duty possible. In addition, they often received furloughs to visit Leonardtown. Hours spent on the beaches, enjoying some sun, swimming, and catching fresh seafood, added enjoyment to their days. According to one veteran, "within a stone's throw of camp, in the river, were enormous oyster beds, from which boat-load after boat-load of luscious bivalves were taken."

The infantry detachments guarding the prisoners were supplemented by an active cavalry camp just north of the prison. Ships of the Potomac Flotilla continually patrolled the waterways surrounding the camp. A visitor noted "the bay and river are regularly patrolled by the Navy boats and several gun boats are regularly stationed on either side of the Point."

Regiments were usually rotated in and out of the camp during 1864 and 1865, causing a fairly high number to act as guards during the war. They included: 5th Massachusetts Colored Cavalry Regiment, 2nd, 5th, and 12th New Hampshire Volunteers, 139th Ohio (a 100 day regiment), 4th Rhode Island, 2nd and 5th U.S. Cavalry (portions), 4th and 36th U.S. Colored Troops (from Maryland), 10th Veteran Reserve Corps, and the 2nd Wisconsin Volunteer Artillery Battery.

This rotation created potential problems. Many men returning from the front were exhausted and it took weeks for them to perform their responsibilities at optimal levels. It also took time for the men to settle in and learn the routine.

Relations between the initial contingent of guards—the New Hampshire troops—and the Southern prisoners were usually professional. They had fought each other on many a battlefield and with that came a grudging mutual respect.

On November 27, 1863, Col. Hoffman requisitioned a number of revolvers for the guards. His rationale was: "A sentinel on post with his musket can only give one shot in case of an attack upon him, but if armed with a revolver it gives him the strength of two or three men without such arms." The request was granted and the pistol became the weapon of choice as the guards walked through the camps at night.

That same day, Gen. Butler responded to a worried Sec. of War, Edwin Stanton who fretted about the ability of the camp to be defended against an attack to free the prisoners. "I am convinced that Point Lookout is one of the best situations and with sufficient capacity to retain and control all rebel prisoners that we have or are likely to have in our hands. It is entirely defensible, owing to its situation, with much less than the present force guarding it, against the attack of the whole of General Lee's army," Butler wrote.

The 2nd and 12th New Hampshire returned to the Army of the Potomac and they were replaced on February 25, 1864 by the 36th U.S. Colored Troops. The impact was immediate and dramatic as both sides harbored grudges. The white troops resented being guarded by former slaves and were not reluctant to tell them. The African American troops showed a distain for the men who had enslaved them.

Confederate prisoner, B.T. Holliday recalled seeing the African American troops for the first time: "It was a bitter pill for Southern men to swallow and we felt the insult very keenly. They were impudent and tyrannical and the prisoners had to submit too many indignities." The African American soldiers commonly told the prisoners: "The bottom rail is now on the top."

After an inspection of the camp on May 20, 1864, Col. Hoffman reported a force of 1,654 men acting as camp guards. They included the following units:

> 5th New Hampshire Infantry – 438 men
> 4th Rhode Island Infantry – 320 men
> 36th U.S. Colored Infantry – 753 men
> 2nd Wisconsin Battery – 119 men
> Assorted cavalry – 24 men

When the last of the New Hampshire troops left camp for active campaigning, they were replaced by another African American unit—the 4th U.S. Colored Troops. This was a period of the war when African American soldiers were not permitted to fight, so they relieved white troops, who were be sent back to the front.

Hoffman reported "The troops appear to be in a good state of discipline, their camps are in excellent condition, and the duty of the post is satisfactorily performed." Because Hoffman expected the arrival of as many as 5,000 additional prisoners, he requested a "regiment of disciplined troops or two regiments of militia added to the guard. "The force here should be strong enough not only to control the prisoners, but to resist any raid which the enemy might be led to undertake, or to detach a command to the Virginia shore in case of necessity." The 5th Massachusetts Colored Regiment was subsequently sent to the camp.

**Shooting of Prisoners**

Several incidents of guards shooting unarmed prisoners were recorded. Author Richard Triebe carefully combed the official records and 50 accounts of life in Point Lookout and found at least 13 prisoners killed and 28 wounded at the hands of prison guards. He admits this number may be high, as some accounts may refer to the same incident. The diaries of two prisoners describe 16 shootings and there were probably many others. Bartlett Malone recorded 11 shootings in the 15 months he was incarcerated: seven prisoners were killed and seven wounded. Seventy-three percent of the shooters involved African American guards; 15% were shot by white guards, and the remaining 12% were shot by guards of unknown race. Curiously, the Official Records of the Civil War lists only four shootings.

Some shootings resulted from escape attempts, others from mistakes, and still others because prisoners angered guards for one reason or another. Talking inside tents or making excessive noise after taps caused at least one guard to fire into a tent, wounding two men. Several others were shot when they were out of their tents at night, attempting to relieve themselves at the tubs. Still others were shot when they wandered too close to the "dead line" but were not first warned to step back, and several were shot when they taunted a guard.

One of the most egregious incidents occurred on March 20, 1864, when L.R. Peyton arrived at the camp. Peyton may have been intoxicated when he became unruly and threw insults at Sergeant Edwin Young of the 2nd New Hampshire Infantry. Young pulled out his pistol and told Peyton to desist. According to a subsequent court of inquiry, "Sergeant Young was urged to this act by profane and insulting language and violent gestures by the said Peyton."

Young was exonerated because, in the words of Col. Hoffman, "he was grossly insulted and defied by a prisoner of war, and it was only after this was persisted in without provocation that he was compelled to vindicate himself and the position he held in a manner which resulted so seriously to the offender."

Brig. Gen. Edward Canby, the Assistant Adjutant-General reviewed the findings and wrote, "This does not seem satisfactory to me . . . the killing was, in my judgment, entirely unjustifiable. The sergeant should be put on trial for murder." It appears the Court of Inquiry's verdict stood and Young was exonerated.

This shooting and others caused Col. Hoffman to write to the District Commander during the spring of 1864, "the shooting of a prisoner, except when compelled by a grave necessity cannot be excused." He went on to write such acts of prisoners in custody "can be considered little less than wanton murder." The shootings apparently continued, again causing the guards to be warned that "wanton and unnecessary shooting at prisoners of war for slight offenses will be severely punished." It is doubtful such shootings were harshly punished. Historian Charles Sanders carefully reviewed records of both armies and found the "execution of only one Civil War soldier for war crimes."

**Other Forms of Discipline**
The camp guards and their officers realized prisoners breaking rules warranted discipline, not only for their own crimes, but also to set an example for others. "Wearing a barrel shirt" was the most common form of discipline. A hole was created in one end of the barrel and the other end was knocked out. Placed over a prisoner's head, it appeared he was wearing a barrel. Affixed to the front of the barrel was the prisoner's crime—thief, dog eater, etc. The prisoner was forced to walk around camp for several hours wearing the heavy barrel around his shoulders.

"Riding the horse" was another form of punishment. Here a prisoner's hands were tied behind his back and he was forced to sit on a sharpened rail for several hours. Minutes felt like hours as wood bore into the prisoner's rear end. An even harsher form of punishment was stringing up a prisoner's thumbs with the tips of his toes just barely touching the ground. If the prisoner tired and attempted to put the soles of his feet on the ground, he would feel excruciating pain extending through his thumbs as they were stretched to an unnatural length. Many men passed out from the severe pain, forcing the guards to cut them down, lest their thumbs be dislocated. This form of punishment was banned by the prison high command, but it continued to occur from time to time.

Prison authorities also deployed a form of punishment called the "sweat box," men were shoved inside for hours in the scorching summer heat without food or water. The long, narrow box had no ventilation and the prisoner could not sit down. He was removed only when on the verge of dying and at least one man did succumb because of this form of punishment.

Barrel shirt punishment

Hanging by the thumbs punishment

CAMP CROSS, POINT LOOKOUT, MD., 1863-64.

A Ship of the Potomac Flotilla. The Flotilla was a hodge-podge of various ships. Lightly armed, they primarily pulled guard duty and were not expected to fight battles with the Confederate Navy.

# Chapter 9
## How Prisoners Could Leave the Prison

Prisoners could leave Point Lookout for several reasons: Being exchanged, taking the oath of allegiance, escaping, or dying. The first three categories will be discussed in this section; Chapter 12 contains information on dying.

### Exchanges

Occasional exchanges of prisoners occurred after the Cartel ended in 1863, and usually involved sick and wounded. On December 17, 1863, Gen. Ben Butler, head of the Department of Virginia and North Carolina (including Point Lookout), was ordered by Maj. Gen. E. A. Hitchcock, Commissioner for Exchange of Prisoners, to work with Confederate authorities on a prisoner swap. Butler followed up on this directive on Christmas Day by informing the South he was willing to exchange 502 prisoners from Point Lookout Prison. He noted, "All, I believe, serviceable men and substantially those longest there in confinement." He went on to explain many prisoners had lost a limb in battle or were in such poor shape they could no longer serve in the South's armed forces.

Sec. of War, Edwin Stanton did not condone this activity, for he wrote to Gen. Butler on January 25, 1864: "You will please suspend your order declaring exchanges, and not allow it to be published or issued until the reason and operation of it is explained to this Department and approved."

Not all the able-bodies men wished to be exchanged because it meant they would be returned to their units in the field. Gen. Marston wrote to Col. Hoffman on October 7, 1863, "There is a large number here who do not desire to be exchanged. Some wish to take the oath of allegiance, and some are willing to enter the naval and a few the military service of the United States. Others, if allowed to take the oath of allegiance, would, I have no doubt, soon find their way into the rebel army."

President Abraham Lincoln visited the camp in December, 1863 with Sec. of War Edwin Stanton, but he never recorded his experiences at the prison that housed more than 10,000 men at the time. He apparently learned many of the prisoners were ready to take the oath of allegiance, if given the chance. He wrote on January 2, 1864, "The Secretary of War and myself have concluded to discharge . . . the prisoners at Point Lookout [in] the following classes:

**First.** Those who will take the oath prescribed in the proclamation of December 8 and, by the consent of General Marston, will enlist in our service.

**Second.** Those who will take the oath and be discharged and whose homes lie safely within our military lines.

A week later, Gen. Butler ordered Gen. Marston to poll every prisoner at Point Lookout. Four questions were to be asked:

**First.** Do you desire to be sent south as a prisoner of war for exchange?

**Second.** Do you desire to take the oath of allegiance and parole, and enlist in the Army or Navy of the United States, and if so in which?

**Third.** Do you desire to take the oath and parole and be sent North to work on public works, under penalty of death if found in the South before the end of the war?

**Fourth.** Do you desire to take the oath of allegiance and go to your home within the lines of the U.S. Army, under like penalty if found South beyond those lines during the war?

Each prisoner who answered affirmatively to one of the questions was to be inscribed in a ledger: "You will adopt the form set forth in this book, and let each signature be witnessed, causing the oath and parole to be read to each man, the questions to be propounded to these men alone and apart from any other rebel prisoner."

By March 11, 1864, Gen. Butler could proclaim that every Point Lookout prisoner was queried. Almost a week later, Gen. Marston wrote to Butler he had prepared a list of 600 prisoners wishing to be exchanged and were convalescents from the hospital. The return of Confederate prisoners thus began. Hiram Williams recorded in his diary on April 16, 1865, "5,000 prisoners to go out of here to-morrow. All living inside of the Federal lines." Others wished to join the Union army (see below).

A batch of prisoners was sent to City Point, Virginia for an equal number of Union prisoners in April, 1864. The men were to be "paroled" so they would not take up arms again against the North. However, Gen. Ben Butler, a strong proponent of keeping the prison population to a minimum was incensed to learn the Confederate authorities considered these men to be "exchanged." Butler wrote to the Sec. of War on May 3, 1864, 'These men will be sent into the field against us, and he [the Confederate Commissioner of Exchange] claims he has the right so to do. . . It is now settled, under General Grant's order that the exchange cannot go on . . . the cartel is entirely annulled."

Reports of conditions at Southern prisoner of war camps hardened the upper levels of the administration. Col. Hoffman wrote to military district commander, Col. A.G. Draper on May 29, 1864, "the discharge of prisoners of war on taking the oath of allegiance or other conditions, are suspended until further orders."

This prohibition did not last long, for about 500 prisoners were put on a steamer and sent to Fortress Monroe in mid-September, 1864. These men were deemed sufficiently disabled not to be able to serve in the Confederate army for at least sixty days, but strong enough to weather the passage. This was apparently not the case as four died during the trip. Later that month another 600 sick or wounded were sent across the Potomac River. Still another group sailed during the end of the first week of October, 1864. These prisoners came from several prisoner of war camps to Point Lookout, where they were retained until transports arrived for the trip to Fortress Monroe. In each case, an equal number of Union soldiers were to make the opposite journey.

There was an ongoing determination of which men would be exchanged. A review of prison ledgers revealed men were identified for exchange on December 25, 1863, and in 1864: March 3, 10, 17, 18; April 27; May 3, 18; October 29, 30; November 1; and in 1865: January 17, February 10, 13, 18, 24; March 15, 17, 28. When a large enough contingent of men was identified, they were put on ships and sent south.

## Oath of Allegiance

Men also had the option of taking the oath of allegiance. Placing their hands on a bible and raising their right hands, the men recited the following oath:

> I _____ do solemnly swear, in presence of Almighty God, that I will henceforth faithfully support, protect, and defend the Constitution of the United States, and the union of states thereunder; and that I will, in like manner, abide by and faithfully support all acts of Congress passed during the existing rebellion with reference to slaves, so long and so far as not repealed, modified, or held void by Congress, or by decision of the Supreme Court, and that I will, in like manner, abide by and faithfully support all proclamations of the President made during the existing rebellion having reference to slaves, so long and so far as not modified or declared void by decision of the Supreme Court; So help me God.

A review of the prison ledger books revealed the number of men taking the oath probably related to the harshness of the weather—some men just gave up resisting and went home. A random selection of three dates showed the number of men taking the oath:

>January 9, 1864: 191 men
>April 12, 1864: 87 men
>June 7, 1864: 25 men

Taking the oath did not mean you could immediately walk out of the prison. Bartlett Malone received his invitation to respond to the four questions on March 1, 1864. He selected the option of taking the oath, receiving a pardon, and returning home. He walked out of the prison a year later—only a few weeks before the end of the war. Those who did not take the oath would remain for several months longer.

Charles Hutt's diary contains a number of references to the oath of allegiance. He wrote in his diary on January 4, 1864, "A great many of the prisoners are taking the Oath of Allegiance to the Yankee government." The following day, he added: "Abe's amnesty proclamation is posted all over camp for the benefit of those who wish to swallow the pill."

The guards and their commanders tried hard to convince prisoners to take the oath. After the war, many survivors claimed the deprivations they experienced were a deliberate way to break their wills to get them to wear an oath. A former prisoner claimed after the Fort Pillow massacre, where scores of unarmed African American soldiers were killed, the prison guards were going to take a drawing for hostages among the prisoners unless they took the oath. This apparently worked as scores agreed and were ultimately sent to serve in the Union armies.

Some guards tried to convince prisoners to take the oath by providing false information, such as the surrender of Lee's army or the collapse of the Confederacy.

## Joining the Union Army

Many men, particularly those from Southern regions less committed to the Confederacy, such as North Carolina, were interested in returning to combat, even if it meant wearing blue uniforms. Lt. F.M. Norcross of the 30th Massachusetts Infantry was sent to the camp after Brig. Gen. Marston wrote to Col. Hoffman on October 7, 1863 of his belief that many prisoners would join the Union army if permitted, and after they were polled several months later. Norcross, who was wounded at Port Hudson, Louisiana, was dispatched to Point Lookout to supervise the recruitment efforts.

"I have nearly a regiment recruited," beamed Gen. Ben Butler on March 11, 1864. About 200 prisoners joined the U.S. Navy that month; the rest formed the nucleus of the 1st U.S. Volunteer Infantry Regiment. These men were called "Galvanized Yankees" by their comrades who stayed the course. They were quickly removed from the prison pens and housed in a separate holding area near the guards' camp until they could be transported to staging depots.

Prisoners who made it known they were going to take the oath were often set upon by their prison-mates. Prisoner J.B. Stamp noted these prisoners were "at all times regarded with contempt by the other prisoners." Charles Hutt recorded in his diary on October 16, 1864: "A great many prisoners are enlisting in the Yankee army—poor fools."

So many men were interested that it took but a short time for the 1,000 men to be identified. An additional 600 men could not be accommodated in the regiment, so they were formed into the 4th U.S. Volunteer Infantry Regiment (see Appendix 1).

Captain Henry Dickinson explained why at least some of the prisoners joined the Union army: Without friends or family on the outside providing food and clothing, the men lived a fairly destitute life. "These sufferings and the bad water made many of the poor fellows desperate, for death stared them in the face daily. When approached by recruiting agents of the Federal Government, and many, very many either enlisted in the army or took the oath of allegiance."

## Escape
As the prison camp matured, it became more difficult for men to escape its embrace. A camp visitor observed "any real attempt to over-power the guards would bring immediate heavy fire from the guard's block house, the

forts and the gun boats." But many men were not deterred, spending countless hours thinking about how they could put the prison behind them. This was a difficult proposition given the water barrier surrounding the camp on three sides and a tall wall on the fourth. Some men fashioned rope ladders they swung over the fence and attempted to put distance between them and the camp via a water or land route. A thorough inspection of the tents followed each escape attempt.

Many of the escape attempts involved the water surrounding the camp and its associated beach privileges. In one incident, two men engaged in a swimming contest. One continued swimming and escaped. It was not uncommon for a barrel or some other box to be floating in the Bay. At least one prisoner dove underwater and surfaced underneath it, finding his way to freedom as it continued bobbing away from the camp. On at least one occasion, prisoners congregated on the beach and the men in the center quickly dug a hole and buried themselves in it, leaving only a small tube sticking up through the sand through which they could breath. When all others returned to the prison and the gates were closed, these prisoners burst from the sand and made their way to safety.

Some prisoners fashioned boats out of cracker boxes, but they were usually found before they could be put to use. Two such boats were found during an inspection on February 14, 1864. In another instance, several prisoners fashioned two canoes out of cracker boxes they could assemble when the time was right. The prison authorities learned of the audacious plot before it could be carried out. Not only did the boats end up in a bonfire, so too did their cracker box house, which was also fired as a lesson to any prisoner attempting such an approach again.

Prison authorities reported 50 successful escapes during the camp's existence. The vast majority—33, occurred during the first few months of the camp's existence when procedures were being developed and the guards were learning their trade.

Taking the Oath of Allegiance at Point Lookout Prison

War-weary President Abraham Lincoln

# Chapter 10
## Military Actions Associated with Point Lookout Prison

### Forays into Virginia

Officers commanding the military contingent at Point Lookout were not content to merely guard prisoners. At least five raids took place across the Potomac River to the Northern Neck of Virginia in 1864. Most were conducted by Col. Alonzo Draper and his 36th U.S.C.T. These raids resulted in the arrest of suspected spies and smugglers, and confiscation of considerable supplies. In one such raid on April 15, 1864, 300 infantry and 50 cavalry, supported by three gun-boats from the Potomac Flotilla, headed across the river to Lower Machodoc Creek in Westmoreland County. They seized $40,000 worth of tobacco from Joseph Maddox, whom they arrested and brought back with them. Several of his out buildings were burned when Confederate soldiers used them to fire at the invading force. Draper and his men also rounded up 50 slaves.

Another raid took place between May 11–14, 1864, when Col. Draper and his men headed to the Rappahannock River. This raid was planned to root out dangerous torpedoes, and a total of nine torpedoes where found. A mill belonging to Henry Barrack was destroyed because he was suspected of being involved in manufacturing the torpedoes. Draper's men ran into a small Confederate force and the two sides skirmished. Five Southerners were killed and an equal number captured. According to Col. Draper, "The colored soldiers would have killed all the prisoners had they not been restrained by Sergeant Price, who is also colored." Union forces also rounded up 33 head of cattle, 22 horses and mules, and several vehicles before again crossing the Potomac River.

Draper again ventured across the river on June 11, 1864, and stayed for ten days, rounding up horses, farming implements, and wagons. Several skirmishes occurred during this period, and Draper returned with 350 head of cattle, 160 horses and mules, and 600 slaves.

## The Johnson-Gilmor Raid to Rescue the Prisoners

The growing number of prisoners so close to the Confederacy caused Robert E. Lee to ponder ways he could re-capture them and integrate them back into his ever-dwindling army. He initially considered a rescue effort during the latter part of 1863, but knew the time was not right for the venture.

With the ascension of U.S. Grant to general-in-chief, all Union armies became much more aggressive during the spring of 1864. Lee's losses mounted and he needed reinforcements. He again looked across the Potomac River and this time decided to put his ideas into action. Lee wrote to President Jefferson Davis outlining the plan: Gen. Jubal Early with approximately 14,000 men would march into Maryland with the intent of capturing Washington.

At the same time, a mounted force of about 1,500 men under Gen. Bradley Johnson, a Marylander, would cut the lines of communication and rail lines around Baltimore and then head south into Southern Maryland. Major Harry Gilmor with 100 men of the 1st and 2nd Maryland Cavalry were spun off to attack the railroad north of Baltimore and divert attention from Johnson's drive toward Point Lookout. A third prong was added to the plan: Commodore John Wood would head for Wilmington, North Carolina, where he would put together a number of armed blockade-runners loaded with 800 men to help neutralize the prison. They would also carry arms and ammunition for freed prisoners.

The plan depended on the success of Gen. Jubal Early's invasion of Maryland. If he were successful, he would draw the Potomac Flotilla from its patrols near Point Lookout and force it north to help defend Washington. This would allow Bradley Johnson to head south with his cavalry and Commodore Wood to head to Point Lookout. After Johnson overwhelmed the camp and the prisoners supplied with arms, Early would move closer to St. Mary's County to affect a rendezvous. If successful, Early's small army would double in size to almost 30,000 men.

A series of events transpired against the plan. First, Jubal Early was unable to capture Washington and a large contingent of Federal troops from the Army of the Potomac forced him to abandon his march south. The plan itself was a poorly kept secret, so the Potomac Flotilla froze in place, rather than moving north. At least five large ships of war were also sent to supplement the Flotilla. These turn of events forced Jefferson Davis to abandon the plan on July 10, 1864.

The prisoners felt a double impact on the aborted attempt. Because the raid was common knowledge, the men felt a deep disappointment about its failure. They also had to endure the impacts. The prison's defenses were strengthened (see below) as additional units arrived to help guard the men. In the future, the number of guards would be doubled, and additional ships patrolled the waterways.

General Jubal Anderson Early

General Bradley Johnson
was among the highest ranking officers commanding Maryland units.
He was tasked with freeing the prisoners at Point Lookout Prison.

Col. Harry Gilmor
was to work in tandem with Gen. Johnson
in freeing the Point Lookout prisoners

# Chapter 11
## The Forts or Redoubts

Aside from the wall surrounding the pens, a 50 feet by 15 feet blockhouse was constructed outside the southwestern corner of the camp. Made of logs with holes through which muskets and cannon could fire, the blockhouse was placed outside the main gate and was oriented to guard the prison from attack.

While many believed the stockade fence would be sufficient to withstand a mass escape attempt, the aborted plan to attack the prison and free the prisoners caused Commissary General of Prisoners, William Hoffman, to rethink his ideas. He wrote to the commander of Point Lookout, Gen. James Barnes, on July 13, 1864, "the conspicuous points for the defense of the depot, or to resist a rising of the prisoners, are the narrow necks of land which connect the Point with the mainland, and by defending these as you propose- by stockade or fieldworks in two lines, armed with artillery, one line to meet an attack from without, the other from within- you place yourself in a position from which only a very large force can dislodge you."

No one at Point Lookout had the expertise to design such works, so engineers were quickly dispatched to the area on July 18, 1864. Their design was completed by July 22, when they requested funds to begin to "procure materials and if possible laborers for commencing defensive works at this point." The works included a circular moat, 20 feet wide and 15 feet deep, filled with water. The dirt removed from the ditch was used to build the walls, which rose 15 – 20 feet high, with a walkway at the top. Ultimately, each wall contained breast-high wooden walls upon which sod was piled to reach the designated height. Four of these fortifications were to be built, with

Fort Lincoln arising on the Potomac River side. Each redoubt was 60 yards square and included platforms to mount four cannon. Fort Lincoln, possibly because of its location adjacent to the Potomac River, coupled with the possibility of attack, had an additional platform for two more cannon. Each redoubt also included ammunition magazines.

Engineers predicted it would cost $1.25 each day for civilian laborers and they would need to be fed and housed because of the prison's isolation. The military contingent was out of the question because of its responsibilities of guarding the prisoners. Many units were undermanned because of various illnesses. Construction inched along and the first redoubt, the one in the middle, was completed on November 3, 1864. Work on the remaining two redoubts continued through the winter. Without options, the engineers began using prisoners-- about 300 toiled in the works each day. Concerns mounted because authorities estimated it was costing approximately $1,000 a month for extra tobacco and whisky for the prisoners. When work halted on May 3, 1865 because of the cessation of the hostilities, three of the four redoubts were completed.

Replica of a portion of Fort Lincoln
The Friends of Point Lookout organization has been instrumental
in reconstructing the Fort and providing educational program

# Chapter 12
## Discipline, Death and Misery

As the prison population grew, so too did the demand for beds in the Hammond General Hospital. They quickly outpaced the hospital's facilities, forcing construction of auxiliary medical facilities. These would treat minor illnesses or be a holding tank until beds became available at the hospital. By November, 1863, the prison's medical facilities consisted of 18 hospital tents, placed in two rows, with a broad street between them. A cook/dining tent was place on one of the sides facing the tents. The men in these facilities were housed on raised bunks with mattresses. At least eight prisoners were detailed to care for the sick. Most of these men were either doctors or had been medical students prior to the war.

Dr. Swalm of the U.S. Sanitation Commission reported in November, 1863 there were 1,208 sick and wounded in Hammond General Hospital. He noted the hospital received about 30 prisoners from the prison's tent hospital each day. Deaths were common, primarily from diarrhea, but most of these men also had pneumonia (see below). He was concerned about the lack of medicines for the sick and wounded. A month later, another report was filed, this one by Surgeon Augustus Clark, Medical Inspector of the Prisoners of War. He reported Hammond General Hospital contained 1,037 patients: 532 Confederates and 505 Union. During the month Clark reported 145 deaths; all but one was a Confederate. This begs the question of whether the prisoners were in such bad shape when they were finally admitted to the hospital that their prognosis was dim or they received substandard care. It appears the latter was not the case.

John Paul of Anson County, North Carolina was the first Confederate prisoner to die at Hammond General Hospital on October 11, 1863. He was a 47 year old farmer who had enlisted in the 32nd North Carolina Infantry.

Many prisoners died each day, whether in Hammond General Hospital, camp hospital, or in camp. The number of dying varied through the year and from year to year. The low was an average of 1.64 prisoners dying each day in November 1864; the high was an average of 9.75 men dying each day in February, 1865.

Overall, illness from chronic diarrhea, caused from tainted water, and from dysentery affected 20,000 prisoners at Point Lookout, with 2,050 official deaths. More than half of all prisoner deaths (56%) resulted from chronic diarrhea/dysentery.

Historian Edwin Beitzell bluntly wrote "the prisoners at Point Lookout died from lack of sufficient food, clothing, blankets, shelter, and medical attention the Federal Government could have provided." In addition to the men's compromised immune systems resulting from factors enumerated by Beitzell, disease spread quickly through the camps because of cramped conditions in tents and the need for men to often "spoon" to keep warm.

The following table enumerates causes of deaths at the prison. Most of the "unknown causes" probably were from diarrhea/dysentery, resulting from poor water quality.

## Table 1: Cause of deaths at Point Lookout Prison

| Cause | Deaths | Percent |
|---|---|---|
| Unknown causes: | 1,075 | 33% |
| Diarrhea | 1,039 | 32% |
| Pneumonia | 299 | 9% |
| Dysentery | 232 | 7% |
| Smallpox | 219 | 7% |
| Scurvy | 165 | 5% |
| Typhoid Fever | 126 | 4% |
| Measles | 44 | 1% |
| Wounds | 38 | 1% |
| Intermittent Fever | 35 | 1% |
| Erysipelas | 25 | 1% |

A large number of Union soldiers also died at Point Lookout. Former Park Superintendent Jerry Sword put the number at 948. Deaths of African American soldiers were estimated to be about 34. He intimates these deaths were among guards and prison personnel, but could have also included some of the wounded at Hammond General Hospital who inevitably died because of inadequate sanitation or the severity of their wounds.

## Diarrhea/Dysentery

The majority of prisoners suffered from diarrhea during their stay at Point Lookout. It was but a symptom of other problems, such as dysentery, tainted food/water, etc. Dysentery was caused by a bacterial infection. Camp conditions created an environment ripe for the spread of this deadly disease. Water pooled because the clay soil did not permit good drainage. It also caused flooding from time to time, but worse, it allowed filthy pools to form containing human waste and filth. Drainage ditches were built, but they did not fully empty and became a breeding ground for disease. Because many men relieved themselves outside their tents, the environment teemed with microorganisms that sickened and killed the men.

## Smallpox

So horrible was this disease and so virulent, a separate isolated section of the prison was devoted to housing the afflicted. In late October, 1863, Gen. Marston complained to Col. Hoffman, "among every lot of prisoners sent from Fort Delaware to this point there have been cases of smallpox. . . [Which] create alarm here among the troops and the citizen employees of the Government." He requested, "no more will be sent here."

At times the number of men with smallpox exceeded the capacity of the special camp for these patients and they were forced to be left in their tents, which helped spread the disease. About 98% of men inflicted with this serious disease contracted it in a four month period from November, 1863 – February, 1864. At least 219 deaths occurred during this time. Many men were inoculated against smallpox, but sometimes the vaccine was tainted, creating large ulcerated sores in the men.

## Scurvy

Eleven days after Marston wired Hoffman about smallpox, he wrote again, this time explaining "many of the prisoners are afflicted with scurvy." The disease strikes when humans do not get enough Vitamin C from fruits and vegetables. While men were getting the calories needed to survive on a diet of carbohydrates and meat, it did not contain the essential vitamins and minerals needed to sustain good health."

Scurvy is a dreadful debilitating disease, but it is preventable. One prisoner contracted scurvy and his "lips were eaten away, jaws became diseased, and teeth fell out." Another wrote "My gums sloughed away from my teeth. With my fingers I could have removed any tooth from my mouth without pain, for they were ready to drop out."

A total of 3,312 cases were reported between September, 1863 and June 1865, with 167 resulting in death. The incidence of the disease appears to have been most serious between Sept. 1863 and early 1864. In his wire, Marston requested permission to purchase vegetables to supplement the men's diet. When the cost of these foods became too high, or they were unavailable, such as during the winter months, the prison authorities distributed vinegar, which apparently had the same positive impact on decreasing the incidence of scurvy.

Professor James Gillispie noted "Officials knew fruit and vegetables were effective preventatives [against scurvy] but increased amounts were rarely, if ever, provided until scurvy was actually reported as a problem." Historian Roger Pickenpaugh concluded, "The results of this neglect were pathetic."

**Other Diseases**
Men often contracted a number of other diseases, such as Measles, Intermittent Fever, and Erysipelas (lesions to skin).

**Lice**
The scourge of every army, as powerful as any enemy in creating misery, was a tiny (3/16 inch) parasite that feasted on the men. There was no way men could not succumb to this parasite, which thrived when humans are housed in close quarters and are not able to regularly bath and wash their clothing. The tiny parasites feed on blood, causing itching and sometimes infection. Some men kept themselves and their clothes clean, but lice remained a problem. It was a losing battle, for even if a prisoner was able to rid himself of lice, it was a sure bet his tent mates remained infected and their offspring gladly made the jump to new territory. Men also believed the vermin hid in cracks and crevices, ready to pounce when the opportunity arose.

James Payton wrote in his diary on October 31, 1864: "Although I change my underclothes every week, the lice worry you all the time…They bother me very much and make you feel mean all the time." A week later he added, "Lice worry you to death." They were in cracks and even washing of bodies and clothes would not get rid of them. "Our blankets are full of them," he wrote. With little to do, the prisoners spent hours combing through their clothes and bodies for these tiny gray critters and their eggs, dispatching any they found.

## Night/Moon blindness

Night blindness was a curious malady affecting about half the prisoners. As the name implied, it usually struck after dark and lasted until the following morning. The cause remains unclear. Some have hypothesized the salty soup mixed with minerals in the water could have caused the phenomenon; others believed it was the intense reflection of the sun off of the ground, the white tents, and the water. It was most prevalent during summer months.

The number of men who became sick, died, and escaped varied through the time the prison was operational. The chart on page 99, while potentially inaccurate, provides trends.

General James Barnes and Staff
Barnes was the last commander of the St. Mary's Military District

## Number of Prisoners; Deaths; Escapes; Sick*

| Month | #Prisoners | #Died | #Escaped | #Sick |
|---|---|---|---|---|
| **1863** | | | | |
| July | 136 | - | - | - |
| August | 1827 | - | 5 (0.2%) | 19 (1.9%) |
| September | 3942 | 14 (0.6%) | 11 (0.3%) | 50 (1.3%) |
| October | 7585 | 23 (0.3%) | 2 (0.03%) | 150 (2.0%) |
| November | 9731 | 119 (1.2%) | 3 (0.03%) | 886 (9.1%) |
| December | 9153 | 158 (1.7%) | 12 (0.1%) | 660 (7.2%) |
| **1864** | | | | |
| January | 8621 | 138 (1.6%) | - | 534 (6.2%) |
| February | 8678 | 128 (1.3%) | - | 539 (6.2%) |
| March | 8480 | 82 (1.0%) | - | 582 (6.9%) |
| April | 6268 | 43 (0.7%) | - | 469 (7.5%) |
| May | 12617 | 24 (0.02%) | 6 (0.05%) | 977 (7.7%) |
| June | 15500 | 105 (0.7%) | 1 (0.01%) | 1400 (9.0%) |
| July | 14747 | 204 (1.4%) | 2 (0.01%) | 1194 (8.1%) |
| August | 11914 | 211 (1.8%) | 2 (0.01%) | 1174 (9.8%) |
| September | 8691 | 110 (1.3%) | 5 (0.06%) | 611 (7.0%) |
| October | 13811 | 111 (0.8%) | 3 (0.02%) | 955 (6.9%) |
| November | 11104 | 52 (0.5%) | - | 973 (8.8%) |
| December | 10702 | 86 (1.5%) | - | 1046 (9.8%) |
| **1865** | | | | |
| January | 11860 | 161 (1.4%) | - | 545 (4.5%) |
| February | 12231 | 223 (1.8%) | - | 776 (6.3%) |
| March | 11332 | 175 (1.5%) | 2 (0.02%) | 580 (5.1%) |
| April | 20110 | 203 (1.0%) | - | 1731 (8.6%) |
| May | 19818 | 324 (1.3%) | - | 1818 (9.2%) |
| June | 18836 | 256 (1.4%) | - | |

This chart is from Edwin Beitzelll's book (page 41). He urges caution in its use as he believed the number of deaths to be underrepresented. Although the table may under-represent some figures, it gives a good overview of how the incidence of deaths and illness waxed and waned through the time the prison was open. Death rates varied from a low of well under 1% of the prison population in May, 1864 to a high of almost 2% in February, 1865. The greatest numbers of deaths occurred toward the end of the prison's existence in May, 1865. Tragically, the war was over at that point.

The incidence of illness also varied during the prison's operation. The last half of 1864 was a particularly difficult period. Nine percent of prisoners were ill in June, 1864 and this rose to almost 10% in August. The illness rates fell in September, but then marched up to almost 10% again in December. These were not minor colds or the flu. As seen in the chart, they were mainly cases of dysentery/diarrhea, smallpox, and scurvy, which could kill. The sick overflowed the camp hospital, sending others into Hammond General Hospital.

A total of 214,865 Southerners were imprisoned in Northern camps and at least 25,976 died. Historian Roger Pickenpaugh believed "the lethargy with which Union officials addressed health concerns in their prisons was inexcusable." Another historian, Charles Sanders, attributed the sharp rise in prisoner deaths and illness to Union government policies. He wrote "conditions in camps reached new lows in the winter of 1864 and the number of prisoners requiring medical attention rose precipitously."

# Chapter 13
## Prison Leadership

All Federal prisoner of war camps were overseen by Col. William Hoffman who reported directly to General Meigs. Hoffman also regularly communicated directly with Sec. of War Edwin Stanton, who had a strong interest in the prison system. With the title of Commissary-General of Prisoners, Hoffman was charged with the security and well-being of the prisoners. His biographer characterized him as "although never brilliant, he was an able and efficient officer" who was also a "stern disciplinarian, who seemed to have memorized the army regulations." Like all of us, Hoffman was a product of his upbringing. He was raised by a father who "scratched for every penny."

When Meigs admonished Hoffman to care for prisoners, but not to spend too much money on them, he took the directive to heart. His biographer believed Hoffman had a "habitual preoccupation, boarding on an obsession, for thrift." Another historian explained "financial concerns outgrew their proper place . . . but Hoffman was not evil; he was narrow. He was unimaginative, humorless, hidebound ... He had extremely strict ideas of duty, obligation, and his own career, and he followed those tenants blindly ... from that came suffering."

Hoffman was promoted to the rank of brigadier general on October 7, 1864 and a week later was booted out of his position as Commissary-General of all Federal prisons. The prison system was now divided into two and he was given the almost meaningless post of overseeing all prisons west of the Mississippi River. There were very few of them. Brig. Gen. Henry Wessells was assigned Commissary-General of all prisons east of the Mississippi River, which were the lion's share of the facilities. Some historians believe Sec. of War Stanton made this change because he viewed Hoffman was too "humanitarian." He may have believed Wessels, a former prisoner himself, would more likely carry out his strict retaliatory orders. This change did not stick, for Wessells proved wanting and was shipped off to supervise a prisoner of war camp and Hoffman regained his post as Commissary-General of all prisons in February, 1865.

Point Lookout was overseen by the head of the St. Mary's Military District. These men were usually civilians prior to the war and knew little about complex administrative tasks, such as running a prisoner of war camp with as many as 20,000 prisoners. Commanders were shuffled in and out of the district, each spending but a few months in Southern Maryland. Just as they became comfortable with the routine and could have become more effective, they were transferred away. Most of these men were reassigned to fighting units.

Many officers were not the most competent men, as they had often failed on the battlefield. Point Lookout became a convenient place for them before being reassigned. Prominent historian William Davis believed problems in prisons had more to do with commander incompetence than malice or apathy. He noted that overseeing a prisoner of war camp "was not, after all, the kind of position which tended to attract either the most gallant or the most able officers." They were cooling their heels as prison commanders until the ever-increasing casualty list called them back into active duty.

Some men were competent, but were recuperating from battlefield wounds or needed some "rest and relaxation." These men did not remain long as they were too valuable and needed to be leading men in battle.

Brigadier General Gilman Marston was the initial commander of the prison complex and the new military district encompassed St. Mary's County. During the spring of 1864, Gen. Marston was transferred to the Army of the James where he was given command of an infantry brigade. Brigadier General E.W. Hincks replaced him as commander of the St. Mary's Military

District. He remained in this position for about two months and then was transferred to the Army of the James, where he was given command of an African American Division. He was replaced by Col. A.G. Draper of the 36th U.S. Colored Infantry, who himself was then replaced by Brig. Gen. James Barnes, the last commander of the St. Mary's Military District. Barnes assumed command in the summer of 1864.

As the prison grew and became more complex, the District Commanders appointed officers to oversee the prison. This began when Gen. Marston placed Captain George Sides of the 2nd New Hampshire Infantry in charge of the prison in 1863. Command of the camp became a revolving door. These men had no experience in running a camp, but were there because that's where their unit was quartered. When the 2nd New Hampshire Volunteer Infantry was sent to the front, Capt. W.T. Hartz of the 15th U.S. Infantry was placed in charge of the camp. He was succeeded by Captain J.N. Patterson and then Maj. H. George B. Weymouth. The camp's final commander was Major A.G. Brady, who was not well liked by some of the prisoners and in fact, in the words of one prisoner, "abhorred by all." The men believed he extracted a share of the profits from the sutlers, who charged exorbitant prices. Like so many other aspects of Point Lookout, there were conflicting ideas about him. A Virginia cavalryman considered him "kind" and called him an "excellent, brave and good soldier."

A leader who appeared to care deeply for the well-being of prisoners was Surgeon James Thompson. The record is replete with his requests for proper food, water, clothes, medicines, and shelter for the prisoners. They understood how much he cared about them. One wrote home about the scurvy problem at the prison on March 1, 1865: "I believe Dr. Thompson, U.S. Surg in charge of camp does all in his power to alleviate their sufferings but he is furnished with neither proper diet nor a sufficiency of medicine to correct the malady."

# Chapter 14
## The End of Point Lookout Prisoner of War Camp

Two seminal events occurred in April, 1865: Robert E. Lee surrendered his Army of Northern Virginia on the 9th, and President Lincoln was assassinated five days later. The prisoners saw an immediate change after the latter event. "The guards were doubled around the prison and the rules were strictly carried out. Soldiers talked and looked as if every Confederate had something to do with the crime."

The urge to resist taking the oath of allegiance began to soften after the fall of Richmond and Lee's surrender. One prisoner wrote during this time the oath was "growing more popular" among the prisoners. Delegations from each state met to discuss the situation. According to prisoner George Nelson, "The surrender of [Gen. Joseph] Johnston's army, together with the voluntary surrender of one or two members of President Davis' Cabinet has combined to force upon us the conclusion that the Southern Confederacy is now a thing of the past." Nelson participated in the Virginia meeting and reported after thoroughly discussing the issue, the group decided "our government no longer existed in fact, therefore our obligation to it were at an end, and our honor could in no way be compromised by a course we might pursue." The following day at roll call, the officers were asked about taking the oath of allegiance—of the 2,300 men present, all but 161 agreed to take the pledge.

When Gen. Joe Johnston surrendered his army on April 26, 1865, the war was all but over. "Now surely, we thought we shall be released in a few days." But this was not the case. Weeks passed, but the men received no word on release. Hiram Williams recorded in his diary on April 16 that camp commander Maj. Allen Brady went to Washington "to see about getting a lot of us out of here." He returned the following day with news the prisoners were going to be released but "owning to Lincoln's assassination, they [the orders] are countermanded."

Days stretched into weeks. April ended and the month of May brought no news. "As each succeeding day arrived, our anxiety and solicitude increased in geometrical proportion," recalled a prisoner. Private John Murphy recorded in his diary on June 12, 1865, "All things looked dark and gloomy. I visited the camps; the boys seem to be in low spirits." Then, a few days later, "glorious news arrived"— the men were to be released on the condition they took the Oath of Allegiance. Thousands who had eschewed taking the oath for more than a year, now reluctantly did so, as the war was over and they were anxious to get home and rebuild their lives. June 21, 1865, was the date of release for Hiram Williams, who had been at Point Lookout only since the beginning of April.

The men were released in alphabetical order, about 500 to 600 a day until all were finally gone. The guards did not simply open the gates—there was a process to be followed. A variety of information on each prisoner was recorded in large ledger books: weight, height, age, state/county of residence, regiment, eye color, hair color, and other characteristics and conditions were noted. "Lastly, you had the iron clad oath administered to you and certificate of release given and you were turned on the outside a free man once more." Private B.T. Holliday would never forget taking the Oath. "We were taken to an adjoining enclosure, where we remain for several days, our names were being enrolled in the books and we signed our parole not to take up arms until exchanged. There was a platform, over the top of which was stretched a large U.S. flag. This platform held standing room for 16 men, and that number was called up at a time. And the oath administered to them." The men were required to place their hands on a bible, which many kissed after taking the oath.

After the men completed this process, "we were turned loose on a green, grassy sward outside of the prison gate, and the men were so wild with joy that old veterans playfully tumbled and rolled on the grass like young schoolboys," recalled George Neese.

Prisoners living in Maryland were permitted to simply walk home. But those, whose destinations were more distant, were gathered together by State and marched onto a transport that delivered them to their destinations. Sometimes, men were forced to wait awhile until there were enough men to fill a steamer. As they marched toward the steamer, "we remembered Lot's wife and never looked back."

The misery was only beginning for most men. Charles Loehr recalled arriving at Richmond, Virginia. "Silent, friendless, and sorrowful each went his own way. No welcome, no cheer awaited their return to the city and to their homes. Oh how few could boast of having homes! Nothing but ruins everywhere..."

The camp officially closed on August 2, 1865 and the buildings were put up for disposal. The public sale of the surplus property, including the wood used to build the facilities began on January 18, 1866. Within the year, all of the buildings had either been sold or torn down. The sales netted a whopping total of $2,845. The prison mess halls netted $655; the ice house, $90, and the laundry, $115. Anything not sold was purchased for pennies on the dollar by William Bayard or sold at public auction in Washington and Baltimore.

Conflict would, however, continue to visit the lowest portion of Southern Maryland. As the war ended and the last prisoner and patient left Point Lookout, a prominent Chicago philanthropist, Delphine Baker, waged her own campaign to establish a disabled veterans' asylum. Her search for an optimum facility ended at Point Lookout. U.S. Grant initially supported the proposal on July 14, 1865, writing, "I see no objection to the use of Point Lookout as a place for temporary use as a Home for Disabled Soldiers. The number of public buildings already there, which are of no further use for public service, makes it, I think, altogether peculiarly appropriate for that purpose." Other voices began questioning whether a former prisoner of war camp was a fitting place to house Union veterans. In January, 1866, the War Department ordered the land sold and the camp dismantled. Ms. Baker was not to be denied, for she purchased 300 acres to house the facility. Unlike others she planned across the country, the one in Southern Maryland never came to fruition.

# Chapter 15
## How Many Prisoners Died at Point Lookout?

Among the most controversial aspects of the prisoner of war camp at Point Lookout is the number of men who died while under the care of the Federal authorities. Gerald Sword, a former park superintendant, conducted considerable research on the prison and noted, "The exact death rate will perhaps never be known due to the poor record keeping systems in use at the time and to the variations in reporting methods." Using a figure of 52,264 men incarcerated during the war, and the official death toll of 2,950, the percentage of prisoners who died was 5.6%. However, the monument to the dead at Point Lookout actually lists 3,384 names or 6.4%.

A cursory review of the records by Richard Triebe uncovered additional deaths, swelling the number to 3,731 or a mortality rate of 7.1%. Members of the Point Lookout Prisoners of War Descendants Organization (PLPOW) assert as many as 14,000 men died at the camp. However, there is not adequate information to back this claim. Not recorded in the official figures were those men who died while being transported home and those who perished while attempting to escape. We will probably never know the actual number of men who died at Point Lookout, but the figure could well be in excess of 4,000. Many more probably lived a substantially shorter life because of the rigors of the camp.

### Burying the Prisoners
Deceased prisoners were buried in three sites. The "Peach Orchard," located just north of the camp, measured 90 feet by 89 feet and contained fewer than 63 bodies. It was used in August, September, and October of 1863.

The actual name of the site is in question as there was not a peach orchard at this site. It may have connoted the bloody battleground at Gettysburg.

Another burial site was near the smallpox hospital north of Point Lookout Creek. At least 1,200 men were interred there. The third area was further north, near Tanner's Creek, where upwards of 3,500 men were buried. These sites probably contained the remains of all who perished at Point Lookout, not just the prisoners. A visitor to the camp noted "their graves are marked with wooden boards with their names, rank and unit marked thereon." Wind and wave action buffeting these areas obliterated the writing on the boards, rendering at least a third unreadable by 1867. A marsh fire sweeping through one of the cemeteries burned the remaining headboards. The bodies lying in the Peach Orchard were reinterred in the other two cemeteries after the camp closed.

While the hospital had a well-developed system for removing the dead and burying them in an expeditious manner, the same may not have been true of the prison. On November 16, 1863, the prison hospital Registrar reported the bodies of three men who had died three days previously were still lying in the prison compound, rapidly decomposing.

The Chesapeake Bay is a greedy mistress, claiming more and more land with each passing year. Confederate graves, often demarked by depressions in the soil, were in danger of being be taken by the Bay. The bodies were exhumed and moved three times until they rested in a large grave site just north of the former prison. Sympathy toward the plight of Confederate dead increased with the years after the war, and the Maryland General Assembly enacted legislation in 1870 for the purchase of up to two acres of land for a new cemetery. A total of $3,000 was allocated and a board of trustees appointed. Another appropriation was sought in 1874 when these initial funds were expended. The request was funded. After land was purchased and the bodies moved to a mass grave, a monument was erected. The new cemetery was dedicated as part of the national Centennial Celebration on July 4, 1876. Once their work was completed, the trustees stopped meeting. Then, in 1909, the trustees met and recommended ceding the cemetery to the Federal

Government. The following year the Federal Government erected another monument to the dead Confederate prisoners. Completed in 1911, the monument rose 85 feet and was composed of reinforced concrete faced with North Carolina granite, at a cost of about $20,000. The original monument was also relocated during this process.

Controversy arose again in 1998 when the Maryland Department of Veterans Affairs ordered the removal of the Confederate flag that had flown there for decades. To counter this action, the Point Lookout Prisoners of War Descendants Organization (PLPOW) purchased a piece of land adjacent to the cemetery. They later commissioned a bronze sculpture of a Confederate prisoner by noted artist Gary Casteel.

The Union dead were also buried near the prison. By 1867, the Union high command was so concerned the graves were often covered with water during high tide that the corpses were dug up and reinterred at new Arlington National Cemetery.

Sign at entrance of Point Lookout

# Chapter 16

## How the North Believed Their Treatment of Point Lookout Prisoners was Justified

A review of Point Lookout camp conditions cannot be undertaken without understanding the political climate. The growing war of words between the two governments, including disagreements about the treatment of African American soldiers and their white officers led to the end of the Cartel system of exchange. Then, during the fall and winter of 1863, reports reached the North of widespread mistreatment of Union soldiers in Southern prisons. General-in-Chief Henry Halleck wrote, "The treatment of our prisoners of war by the rebel authorities has been even more barbarous than that which Christian captives formerly suffered from the pirates of Tripoli, Tunis and Algiers." He went on to write, "it has been proposed to retaliate upon the enemy by treating his prisoners precisely as he treats ours. Such retaliation is fully justified by the laws and usages of war."

The South did experience problems in caring for the Northern prisoners. It did not help that the Confederate government did not appoint a "Commissioner of Prisons," a position similar to Col. Hoffman's until close to the end of the war, and this weakened the prison officials' ability to effect widespread change and get the resources they needed. According to historian James Gillispie, the South hoped for a resumption of prisoner exchanges which would empty their prisoner of war camps. Most modern authors argue the Confederate government did not intend to mistreat prisoners—it was more of a "benign neglect." The men in these positions cared deeply for their charges and desperately tried to improve their living conditions, but they were unable to get support from the highest levels of government. For example, despite their pleas, Commissary General, Col. Lucius Northrop, ended all meat rations to prisoners housed in Richmond prisons in October, 1863 and this continued for several weeks. Days without meat were not uncommon. Edward Pollard, the editor of the *Richmond Examiner*, was present during a heated exchange between Northrop and prison official, Gen. William Winder. "I know nothing of Yankee prisoners," Northrop allegedly proclaimed, "throw them all into the James River!" The increasing hostility between these men did nothing to improve the situation of Yankee prisoners.

Secretary of War Edwin Stanton was outraged by reports of the mistreatment of Northern prisoners, and he wrote to Gen. E.A. Hitchcock, the Commissioner of Exchange on November 9, 1863: "you are directed to take measures for precisely similar treatment toward all the prisoners held by the United States, in respect to food, clothing, medical-treatment, and other necessities." Gen. Hitchcock immediately counseled against such a move for it would potentially cause uprisings in camps such as Morton and Chase which had inadequate security forces. Stanton relented, but other, less severe retaliatory measures were taken. On November 23, Col. Hoffman announced prisoners could no longer receive packages from anyone other than immediate family members. No longer could they benefit from "disloyal friends and sympathizers." The following week, all sutlers were told to leave the camps, on Christmas Eve, he cut the molasses rations by three-fourths.

Believing conditions had improved in Southern prison camps by late winter, 1864, Stanton ordered the restrictions relaxed. Hoffman allowed sutlers to return on March 3, 1864 (although he was given authority to do so on December 29, 1863). It came with the proviso that only certain items could be stocked and sold, such as undergarments and shoes, but no outerwear. Vegetables, meats, and fish could be sold. Eight days later, Hoffman again allowed packages, but they could contain "nothing harmful or contraband."

The reprieve was short-lived, for continued reports of Union prisoner mistreatment surfaced. Stanton ordered Col. Hoffman to see the situation for himself, so he traveled down to Annapolis, the initial destination point for exchanged sick soldiers. He reported "some of these poor fellows were wasted to mere skeletons and had scarcely life enough remaining to appreciate they were now in the hands of friends . . . Many faces showed that there was scarcely a ray of intelligence left." He concluded that our soldiers "when in the hands of the rebels are starved to death cannot be denied." His recommendation: "retaliatory measures be at once instituted by subjecting the officers we now hold as prisoners of war to a similar treatment." Photographs were taken of the worst cases and distributed throughout the North and reporters were invited to observe the returning men, resulting in scathing articles about Southern cruelty. This had the desired effect of creating a public uproar supporting the implementation of progressively harsh reprisals against Southern prisoners, beginning in the spring of 1864. According to author Charles Sanders, these actions were "deliberately designed to lower conditions in the camps and increase immeasurably the suffering of the prisoners."

There were indeed problems in securing supplies in the South. The ever-tightening Union blockade prevented goods from entering the ports, and continued loss of territory because of Union victories, sapped the Confederacy of food needed to nourish it citizens, its armies, and the prisoners. A food riot broke out in Richmond during the winter of 1864-65 and Robert E. Lee's men were on a starvation diet, being forced to scrounge for edible weeds to supplement their meager diet. However, Charles Sanders in his book, *While in the Hands of the Enemy*, argued there was adequate food for all in the South, but distribution problems and a recalcitrant Commissary Department caused civilians, soldiers, and prisoners to suffer.

Only one action could guarantee the well-being of all prisoners-- resumption of a robust exchange system. The South desperately wanted to be rid of prisoners it knew it could not adequately care for, and the Northern population clambered for it. But U.S. Grant's "arithmetic" carried the day.

This was now total war, and Grant would not risk set-backs in the field because Confederate armies were being swelled in numbers by returning prisoners. So, the death and misery continued.

# Chapter 17
## Point Lookout after the War

The vision of a resort again surfaced after the war as speculators bought up land, but a planned railroad never materialized, killing the project. The idea again resurfaced in the late 1920's using cars as a way to get potential buyers to their cottages. A large hotel was built and the area did fairly well as a vacation destination. The opening of the Bay Bridge in 1952 and the ease of getting to Ocean City and the Eastern Shore hurt business. This, combined with the relentless erosion along the Bay, caused the hotel to close.

The State began purchasing land for a park in the 1960's, partly to encourage tourism in an area losing income from slot machines. Governor, J. Millard Tawes hoped the park would help the Southern Maryland economy.

The hand of nature and man were not kind to the forts or redoubts of Point Lookout. The fort adjacent to the Chesapeake Bay (Redoubt #3), was partially destroyed when a power plant was built. The Chesapeake Bay has now claimed it. The fort in the middle (Redoubt #1) was located along the west side of Route 5. Its walls were clearly visible as late as 1937, but were leveled by the Works Project Administration (WPA) shortly thereafter.

Only Redoubt #2 (Fort Lincoln) remains. It was unnoticed and forgotten until 1973 when a State archeologist was asked to investigate an unusual depression. Some wood beams were excavated, but nothing was done with the site. When the owner of the property, Walter Tuckerman, realized what the site represented, he deeded the 4.25 acres of land to St. Mary's County Government. Part of the requirements of his donation included a provision for a public park so others could appreciate its significance. The County reneged on this agreement and the land reverted back to Tuckerman's heirs. They subsequently deeded the property to the State of Maryland on September 29, 1967.

Soon after, Fort Lincoln found its way to public lands. However, when the Potomac River set its eyes on the fort's west walls, causing erosion, the State immediately took action, placing a massive rock revetment along the endangered area. Work then began in earnest to remove the vines and brush that covered the walls of the fort and in 1981, the Youth Conservation Corps and park employees began the process of reconstructing the fort. They were aided by the original plans dating back to February 20, 1865.

The Friends of Point Lookout has taken up the mission of restoring and preserving Point Lookout since the 1980's. The group has restored every building at Fort Lincoln and reconstructed the parapet and prison pen gate. The Friends also helped create and maintain the Civil War museum and small research library at the Visitor Center at Point Lookout State Park. The group also performs living history programs at Point Lookout and work with the school system to give tours to groups from local schools. This group has done yeoman service in helping to keep the memory of Point Lookout Prisoner of War camp alive.

**A Final Thought**
We entered this project with much trepidation as the "battle lines" were well drawn between those who believed the Federal authorities were effective caregivers doing their best to provide for the prisoners and those who felt they did just enough not to kill the prisoners. We tried to take an impartial approach, as can be seen in this book's Introduction. However, in the end, we believe the care provided to the prisoners could have been much better. We are struck by the constant communications between high ranking U.S. officials who retaliated against the South by reducing the prisoners' rations and only begrudgingly providing them with clothes and blankets, often unacceptable for their own soldiers.

Sec. of War Stanton appeared to have little sympathy for the well-being of Confederate prisoners under his care. Time and time again his communications revealed a callous disregard for human life. The Union officers tasked with overseeing the prisoners often did their best to advocate for the men under their care, but their voices were often ignored. Curiously, most biographies of Stanton fail to describe his role in eliminating prisoner exchanges and his role in the worsening conditions in Union prisoner of war camps.

Massive numbers of men incarcerated at the Point Lookout Prison made providing supplies a logistical nightmare. During the height of the winter of 1864-65 there were as many as 11,000 prisoners housed in the camp. This meant the supply agents needed to send at least 11 cords of wood each day Point Lookout. Given the resources of the Federal Government, it is hard to understand why each man could not have been provided with at least one stick of wood each day. Combined with those of tent-mates, they may have been able to build and maintain adequate fires in their tents to help ward away the bone chilling cold. The same could be said about clothing, blankets, and food. The resources were there—it simply required the will to provide them, but anger over the treatment of Union soldiers in Southern prisons called for retaliation.

Other issues were involved, and even Professor James Gillispie, who painted the Union treatment of the prisoners in a positive light, agreed the Federal government could have done a better job. In addition to poor leadership, he believed "the most glaring and consistent problem with Northerners' management of their prisoner of war facilities, was their failure to anticipate potential problems and deal with them as effectively as possible before they became serious."

The Point Lookout Prisoner of War Camp is a major part of Southern Maryland's history. We must always remember what happened there, not to celebrate one side or the other, but as a testament to man's ability to weather adversity. Charles Sanders probably summed up the situation best when he ended his seminal book on Civil War prisoner of war camps with the statement: "the treatment of prisoners during the American Civil War can only be judged as 'a most horrible national sin.'"

Confederate memorial outside of Point Lookout State Park

# Appendix 1
## The Galvanized Yankees

In an effort to reduce the prison population without sending former soldiers back to their units, President Lincoln and Secretary of War Stanton developed a plan to ask four questions relating to their willingness to be released or to serve in the Union armed forces. The questioning at Point Lookout began in January and extended into late March 1864. During the latter part of that month, Gen. Ben Butler wrote to Sec. of War Edwin Stanton, "more than a minimum regiment of repentant rebels, whom a friend of mine calls 'transfugees,' recruited at Point Lookout. They behave exceedingly well, are very quiet, and most of them I am certain are truly loyal, and I believe will make as efficient a regiment as there is in the service. I would like to organize and arm it at once."

Point Lookout prisoners who took the oath of allegiance and volunteered for the Union army were mustered into the 1st U.S. Volunteer Infantry Regiment. A second regiment, the 4th U.S. Volunteer Infantry Regiment, was also formed from Point Lookout prisoners. A total of six regiments, totaling 6,000 men were ultimately recruited from all of the Northern camps.

According to author Michele Butts, men threw their lot with the Union forces for a variety of reasons, including, "war weariness, limited commitment to 'the cause,' Unionist sentiment, class resentments, and hardships at home." There were other incentives, such as "escape from the horrors of prison life, Union greenbacks, and protection for his loved ones within Union lines." Many men who took up this opportunity tended to be from the areas of the South with mixed sentiments, such as Tennessee and North Carolina.

A group of 1,000 prisoners boarded the convoy ship, *George Henry*, in late April, 1864, heading for Norfolk Virginia, where they performed guard duty. They were now the 1st U.S. Volunteer Infantry Regiment. Gen. Butler sent the regiment on a raid to Elizabeth City, North Carolina, which did not amount to much. However, the event caught the attention of Gen. U.S. Grant. Concerned about their actual loyalties, and what would happen to them if captured, he was not in favor of keeping them in the South. On August 9, 1864, he informed the War Department he was sending the unit west.

Manpower was desperately needed by Maj. Gen. John Pope, who commanded the Department of the Northwest. A series of forts were being constructed along the Dakota frontier to protect steamboat passages and over-land route travelers from Sioux Indians. The 1st U.S. Volunteer Infantry Regiment served from 1864 through the end of the war. About 400 men were sent to the Minnesota-Dakota frontier; the other 600 built and garrisoned Fort Rice in Dakota Territory on the upper Missouri River.

Life on the frontier did not prove to be much better than the prisoner of war camp. During the winter of 1864-65, the men sustained brutal weather with temperatures often well below zero. Men who believed their diets would improve were sadly mistaken, as scurvy and other nutritional diseases plagued the men. Twenty-nine "Galvanized Yankees" perished that winter.

Realizing the threat posed by new settlers, the Sioux struck back, forcing the men of the 1st U.S. Volunteer Infantry into periodic fights. At least eight men were killed and several others wounded. They helped to beat off at least one determined attack on Fort Rice. With the end of the Civil War, the Galvanized Yankees expected to be mustered out of service and permitted to go home. This was not the case and their terms of service did not end until May, 1866.

Ben Butler received permission to recruit a second regiment from Point Lookout prison in October, 1864. Only six companies were formed and the men who served were considered to be of a poorer quality than those who volunteered for the 1st U.S. Volunteer Infantry Regiment. They shipped out on April 30, 1865 and reached the west in May. The unit was divided and garrisoned three forts in the Dakotas. The regiment was not mustered out of service until June, 1866.

Major General John Pope
Commanded the Department of the Northwest

Major General Benjamin Butler
was influential in developing and implementing the concept
of the "Galvanized Yankees"

Assistant Adjutant-General, Brigadier General Edward Canby
One of his responsibilities was ensuring proper
military disciplinary actions were being carried out

Confederate Soldier Memorial Today

# Appendix 2
## The Fall and Rise of Prisoner Exchanges and Paroles

Sec. of War Edwin Stanton was probably the architect of the end of the exchange system, blaming Confederate "cheating" as the cause. During the late summer of 1863, he moved to terminate exchanges completely, using the rationale of being worried prisoners were returning to the Confederate army before being formally exchanged. According to historian Charles Sanders, Stanton "demonstrated he had no qualms about ignoring the Union's own regulations if he perceived an advantage in doing so." The North's Agent for Exchange, Lt. Col. William Ludlow, did not agree with Stanton and protested the action, only to be quickly removed from his position.

Execution of some prisoners, particularly by the North, also brought rancor. The issue of the treatment of black soldiers, commanded by white officers, was also a major source of contention. The Confederacy informed the U.S. Government it would refuse to treat black soldiers the same as whites and if captured could be sold into slavery or put to death along with their white officers. This infuriated Sec. of War Edwin Stanton. Historian Charles Sanders posited that Jefferson Davis promulgated this policy to prevent the North from enlisting thousands of new troops into the Union army's ranks. Stanton was not to be dissuaded and to protect these men, he countered by threatening to end the entire cartel, hoping to soften Southern policy toward black soldiers and their white officers.

Realizing his country could not adequately care for thousands of Union prisoners; President Jefferson Davis dispatched his vice president, Alexander Stephens, to seek a meeting with President Abraham Lincoln in June, 1863 to attempt to get the discussions on exchanges back on track. Lincoln refused to meet with Stephens, and the twin victories at Gettysburg and Vicksburg, strengthened Lincoln's hand. News of the end of the Cartel created an uproar in the North. Stanton merely noted it was the South's fault, laying the blame on "Rebel deceit and vengefulness."

While U.S. Grant was not involved in the initial decision to end the Cartel system as he had his hands full trying to capture Vicksburg Mississippi during 1863, he was instrumental in keeping it suspended after he assumed the all-powerful position of General-in-Chief early in 1864. To Grant, it was all about arithmetic. The much larger north, with a supply of African Americans willing to serve, had an almost unlimited number of men to fight; the South was more limited, and as the war dragged on, it became harder to replace those lost in battle. According to Grant, why assist the enemy by helping to restock his army with prisoners. He wrote, "If we hold those caught they amount to no more than dead men."

Some exchanges occurred after mid-July 1863, but they mainly involved the sick and wounded—men neither side wished to be responsible for. This led to a mushrooming of prison populations in the North and South. The North held 1,286 captives in January, 1863, but because of the dissention between the two governments, the numbered ballooned to almost 35,000 by the end of the year. According to a recent author, "With the stroke of a pen, prisons transitioned from temporary detention centers to long-term prisons . . . Thousands of soldiers on both side who had served their respective countries in battle wound up fighting for their own lives in prisoner of war camps."

While the exchange of prisoners resumed in early 1865, the 15 months without it created horrible conditions in both Northern and Southern prisons. Prison populations soared and thousands needlessly died or lived and never recovered physically or emotionally.

# Bibliography

A number of seminal works describe the history and conditions of the Point Lookout Prisoner of War Camp. The *Official Records of the Civil War* contains the myriad dispatches and reports dealing with the prison. *The Chronicles of St. Mary's*, published by the St. Mary's Historical Society is filled with important accounts and analyses. Many former prisoners recounted their experiences in a number of articles in the *Southern Historical Society Papers* and in the *Confederate Veteran Magazine*.

The following are books the reader might wish to consult for additional information. The two most important works are those by Beitzell and Triebe.

Beitzell, Edwin W. *Point Lookout Prison Camp for Confederates*. Abell, MD: Published by author, 1983.

Benson, Berry. *Berry Benson's Civil War Book: Memoirs of a Confederate Scout and Sharpshooter*. Susan Williams Benson, ed. Athens, GA: The University of Georgia Press, 1992.

Brown, D. Alexander. *The Galvanized Yankees*. Urbana, IL: University of Illinois Press, 1963.

Burnham, Philip. *So Far From Dixie: Confederates in Yankee Prisons*. Lanham, MD: Taylor Trade Publishing, 2003.

Butts, Michele. T. "Trading Gray for Blue: Ex-Confederates Hold the Upper Missouri for the Union. *Prologue Magazine*, vol. 27, no. 4 (2005).

Cloyd, C. Benjamin. *Haunted by Atrocity: Civil War Prisons in American Memory*. Baton Rouge, LA: Louisiana State University Press, 2010.

Davis, William C. *Rebels and Yankees: The Fighting Men of the Civil War*. New York: Salamander Books, 1989.

Dickinson, Henry C. *Diary of Captain Henry C. Dickinson, C.S.A.* Denver, CO: Press of Williamson & Haffner, Co., n.d.

Gillispie, James M. *Andersonvilles of the North: The Myths and Realities of Northern Treatment of Civil War Confederate Prisoners.* Denton, TX: University of North Texas Press, 1911.

Holt, David. *A Mississippi Rebel in the Army of Northern Virginia.* Thomas D. Cockrell and Michael B. Ballard, eds. Baton Rouge, LA: Louisiana State University Press, 1995.

Keiley, A.M. *In Vinculis or The Prisoner of War Being the Experiences of a Rebel in Two Federal Pens Interspersed with Reminiscences of the Late War.* New York: Blelock & Co., 1866.

King, John R. *My Experience in the Confederate Army and in Northern Prisons.* Clarksburg, W.V: United Daughters of the Confederacy, 1917.

King, Julia A. *Archeology, Narrative, and the Politics of the Past: The View from Southern Maryland.* Knoxville, TN: The University of Tennessee Press, 2012.

Malone, Bartlett Yancey. *Whipt'em Everytime: The Diary of Bartlett Yancey Malone.* Jackson, Tennessee: McCowat-Mercer Press, Inc., 1960.

Pickenpaugh, Roger. *Captives in Gray: The Civil War Prisons of the Union.* Tuscaloosa, AL: The University of Alabama Press, 2009.

Sanders, Charles W. *While in the Hands of the Enemy: Military Prisons of the Civil War.* Baton Rouge, LA: Louisiana State University Press, 2005).

Speer, Lonnie. *War of Vengeance: Acts of Retaliation Against Civil War POW's.* Mechanicsburg, PA: Stackpole Press, 2002.

Swank, Walbrook D. *Stonewall Jackson's Foot Cavalry: Company A, 13th Virginia Infantry.* Shippensburg, Pennsylvania: Burd Street Press, 2001.

Toney, Marcus B. *The Privations of a Private*. Tuscaloosa, AL: University of Alabama Press, 2005.

Toomey, Daniel Carroll. *The Johnson-Gilmor Raid- July 9 – 13, 1864*. Baltimore, MD: Toomey Press, 2005.

Triebe, Richard H. *Point Lookout Prison Camp and Hospital*. n.p.: Coastal Books, 2014.

Wynne, Lewis N. Wynne and Robert A. Taylor, *This War So Harrible: The Civil War Diary of Hiram Smith Williams*. Tuscaloosa, Alabama: The University of Alabama Press, 1993).

# Index

Alexander, Dr. C.T., 39, 42

Allen, William, 6

Andersonville Prisoner of War Camp, 1, 2, 3

Annapolis, MD, 26

Antietam, Battle of, 12

Arlington National Cemetery, 109

Army of Northern Virginia, 104

Army of the James, 102, 103

Army of the Potomac, 72, 74, 89

Atlanta Campaign, 24


Baker, Delphine, 106

Bayard, William, 106

Baltimore, MD, 24

Barnes, Gen. James, 46, 51, 91, 103

Beitzell, Edwin, 94, 100

Belle Plain, VA, 28

Benson, Barry, 38

Butler, Gen. Benjamin, 31, 45, 62, 73, 79, 80, 81, 84, 117, 119, 120

Blunt, Sarah, 78

Bowden, Malachi, 65

Brady, Maj. A.G., 44, 49, 103, 105

Bunton, Dr., 58

Butts, Michele, 117

Cameron, Simon, 12

Camp Chase, 3

Camp Cross, 72, 78

Camp Morton, 3

Camp Douglas, 3

Canby, Gen. Edward, 76, 120

Cartel, 13, 79, 81, 110

Casteel, Gary, 109

Chesapeake Bay, 5, 18, 41, 63, 72, 85, 108, 113

Chicago, IL, 106

City Point, VA, 51

Clark, Dr. Augustus, 93

College of William and Mary, 65

*Commodore Foote*, 42

Conlan, Sr. Consolata, 7

Cross, Col. Edward, 72


Danville, VA, 27

Davis, Jefferson, 89, 104, 122

Davis, William, 102

Davidson, Kath, 26

Davidson, Mrs. Hunter, 26

Diarrhea/Dysentery, 41, 42, 47, 56, 93, 94, 95, 100

Dickinson, Capt. Henry, 9, 29, 37, 40, 50, 84

Draper, Maj. Alonzo, 81, 87, 88, 103

Early, Gen. Jubal, 88, 89

Edwards, Capt. L.C., 7

Elizabeth City, NC, 118

Elmira Prison, 3, 33

Erysipelas, 95, 97

Fitchburg, MA, 27

Fort Delaware, 3, 18, 24, 26

Fort Lincoln, 92, 113, 114

Fort Pillow, 83

Fort Rice, 81

Fortress Monroe, 81

Friends of Point Lookout, 114

"Galvanized Yankees," 19, 84, 117, 118, 120

*George Henry*, 118

Gettysburg, Battle of, 14, 108, 123

Gillispie, James, 1, 3, 42, 97, 110, 115

Gilmor, Maj. Harry, 88, 90

Gilliam, Mary, 26

Grant, Gen. U. S., 81, 88, 106, 118, 123

Haigh, William, 50

Hall, James, 39

Halleck, Gen. Henry, 14, 15, 110

Hammond, Dr. W. A., 6, 7, 10

*Hammond, The Gazette*, 9

Harpers Ferry, WV, 12

Hartz, Capt. W.T., 103

Harwood, Commodore A.A., 14

Hincks, Gen. E.W., 102

Hitchcock, Gen. E.A., 15, 79, 111

Hoffman, Col. William: As Commissary-General of Prisoners: 12, 101, 102, 110; Early period of prison: 14, 15, 21, 24, 26; Response to Swalm report: 32, 35; Food: 33, 34, 36, 37, 40; Clothing: 43, 44, 45, 46; Blankets: 52; Packages: 61, 62, 111; Work details: 65; Spirituality: 69; Guarding the prisoners: 73, 74, 76, 91; Prisoner release: 79, 81, 84

Holliday, B.T., 16, 50, 74, 105

Holt, David, 28, 45, 60

Hopkins, Luther, 41

Hutt, Charles, 38, 40, 44, 53, 67, 83, 84

*Ide*, 42


James River, 111

Johnson, Gen. Bradley, 88, 90

Johnson Island Prison, 3, 24

Johnson, William Cost, 6

Jones, C.W., 38

Jones, Freeman, 41

Johnston, Gen. Joseph, 104


Keiley, Anthony, 37, 41, 51

Kern, Joseph, 69

King, John, 60

Lee, Gen. Robert E., 2, 12, 88, 104, 112

Leon, Lewis, 17

Leery, John, 9

Libby Prison, 2

Lice, 63, 97

Lincoln, Abraham, 80, 86, 117, 122, 123

Loehr, Charles, 106

Lower Machodoc Creek, 87

Ludlow, Lt. Col. William, 122


Maddox, Joseph, 87

McLaughlin, J., 9

Malone, Bartlett, 38, 45, 51, 53, 54, 67, 75, 123

Marston, Gen. Gilman: Camp's early days: 15, 21, 72, 103; Response to the Swalm report: 32, 35, 43, 44, 48, 52, 55, 56, 57; Food: 33, 34, 35; Spirituality: 69, Prisoner release: 79, 80, 81, 83; Disease: 33, 96; Leaves post: 102

Maryland Units: 1st Cavalry, 88; 2nd Cavalry, 88

Massachusetts Units: 5th Colored Infantry, 73, 75; 9th Infantry; 9; 30th Infantry, 83

Meade, Gen. George, 72

Meigs, Gen. Montgomery, 7, 9, 12, 20, 36, 42, 101

Mississippi River, 101, 102

Mobile, AL, 46

Murphy, John, 105


Neese, George, 38, 42, 53, 59, 105

Nelson, George, 104

New Hampshire Units: 2nd Infantry, 58, 72, 73, 74, 75; 5th Infantry, 19, 72, 73, 74, 103; 12th Infantry, 72, 73, 74

Night Blindness, 98

Norcross, Lt. F.M., 83

Norfolk, VA, 118

Northrup, Col. Lucius, 111

Nutt, Charles, 59

Ohio Units: 139th Infantry, 73

Old Capitol Prison, 15, 26, 27

Overland Campaign, 24

Patterson, Capt. J. N., 103

Paul, John, 94

Payton, James, 38, 45, 52, 53, 54, 61, 64, 65, 66, 67, 68, 97

Payton, L. R., 75

Peach Orchard, 107, 108

Perkins, Jane, 27

Pickenpaugh, Roger, 36, 97, 100

Pollard, Edward, , 111

Pope, Gen. John, 118, 119

Port Hudson, LA, 84

Potomac Flotilla, 14, 73, 78, 88, 89

Potomac River, 5, 7, 26, 41, 42, 47, 72, 82, 92, 114

Pt. Lookout Prisoner of War Descendant Organization, 107, 109

Rappahannock River, 87

Revolutionary War, 5

Rhode Island Units: 4th Infantry, 1, 2, 63, 67, 73, 74

Richmond, VA, 27, 106, 111

Rock Island Prison, 3


Sanders, Charles, 3, 76, 100, 112, 115, 122

Scurvy, 34, 36, 37, 40, 61, 95, 96, 100

Seward, William, 9

Sides, Capt. George, 103'

Sisters of Charity, 7

Smallpox, 96, 100

Smith, Alfred, 53

Speer, Lonnie, 39

Stamp, J.B., 16, 28, 84

Stanton, Edwin: Cartel/prisoner release: 13, 79, 80, 117, 122, 123; Treatment of prisoners: 15, 20, 36, 39, 44, 61, 70, 73, 101, 102, 111,

Stevens, Alexander, 122, 123

Swalm, William: Report on hospital: 32, 56, 57, 93; report on prison conditions: 33, 34, 35, 36, 41, 43, 48, 49, 52, 55,

Sword, Gerald, 95, 107


Tanner's Creek, 108

Tawes, Gov. J. Millard, 113

Thompson, Dr. James, 24, 37, 103

Toney, Marcus, 61

Triebe, Richard, 75, 107

Tuckerman, Walter, 113


United States Units: 1st Volunteers, 84, 1217, 118, 119; 2nd Cavalry, 73; 5th Cavalry, 73; 4th Volunteers, 84, 117; 15th Infantry, 103

United States Colored Troops (USCT): 4th Infantry; 36th Colored, 73, 74, 87, 103

U. S. Naval Yard, 14


Veteran Reserve Corps Units: $10^{th}$, 73

Vicksburg, Battle of, 14, 123


War of 1812, 5

Washington

Wells, Gideon, 14

Wessells, Gen. Henry, 101, 102

Westmoreland County, VA, 87

Weymouth, Maj. H. George, 103

White, Father Andrew, 5

Wilkinson, J.H., 35, 36

Williams, Hiram, 60, 81, 104, 105

Wilmington, NC88

Winder, Gen. William, 111

Wisconsin Units: 2nd Volunteer Artillery Battery, 73, 74

Wood, Comm. John, 88

Young, Sgt. Edwin, 75

Youth Conservation Corps, 114

# About the Authors

### Bradley M. Gottfried, Ph.D.

Brad combines a long and distinguished career of outstanding leadership in higher education with an expertise of the American Civil War. After receiving his Ph.D. from Miami University, Brad became a full-time, tenured professor at the college level for eleven years before entering higher education administration. He ultimately served as President Chief Executive Officer of three colleges (University of Wisconsin-Fond du Lac, Sussex County Community College, and College of Southern Maryland) for almost 25 years. Gottfried has received a number of national and regional awards and recognitions. Brad retired in 2017 and is devoting his life to the study of the Civil War and the traits of effective leaders.

As an historian, Brad has authored twelve books and two additional works are moving through the editorial process. Among his Gettysburg titles are: *Roads to Gettysburg, The Artillery of Gettysburg, The Battle of Gettysburg: A Guided Tour, The Brigades of Gettysburg, and the Maps of Gettysburg.*

### Linda I. Gottfried

Linda retired from a notable twenty-five year career in public relations and fundraising. She has a passion for helping nonprofit organizations achieve their strategic and fundraising goals serving as a keynote speaker and providing pro bono education and training.

Linda earned a B.F.A. in design from William Paterson University and continued her art education in clay becoming an award-winning ceramic artist. Linda is the author of two children's books and this publication is her first foray into the world of American history. Together with Brad they are the proud parents of two sons, two daughters and six grandchildren.

Made in the USA
Middletown, DE
08 September 2025